RENAISSANCE

VOLUME 7

Michelangelo — Palaces and Villas

GROLIER
EDUCATIONAL

Published by Grolier Educational
Sherman Turnpike
Danbury, Connecticut 06816

Set ISBN 0-7172-5673-1
Volume 7 ISBN 0-7172-5669-3

Library of Congress Cataloging-in-Publication Data

Renaissance.
     p. cm.
Summary: Chronicles the cultural and artistic flowering
known as the Renaissance that flourished in Europe and
in other parts of the world from approximately 1375 to
1575 A.D.
Includes index.
Contents: v. 1. Africa–Bologna — v. 2. Books and libraries–
Constantinople — v. 3. Copernicus–Exploration — v. 4.
Eyck–Government — v. 5. Guilds and crafts–Landscape
painting — v. 6. Language–Merchants — v. 7. Michelangelo–
Palaces and villas — v. 8. Palestrina–Reformation — v. 9.
Religious dissent–Tapestry — v. 10. Technology–Zwingli.
  ISBN 0-7172-5673-1 (set : alk. paper)
  1. Renaissance—Juvenile literature. [1. Renaissance.]
I. Grolier Educational (Firm)
  CB361 .R367 2002
  940.2'1—dc21
                                    2002002477

For information address the publisher:
Grolier Educational, Sherman Turnpike,
Danbury, Connecticut 06816

FOR BROWN PARTWORKS

Project Editor: Shona Grimbly
Deputy Editor: Rachel Bean
Text Editors: Chris King
                       Jane Scarsbrook
Designer: Sarah Williams
Picture Research: Veneta Bullen
Maps: Colin Woodman
Design Manager: Lynne Ross
Production: Matt Weyland
Managing Editor: Tim Cooke
Consultant: Stephen A. McKnight
                       University of Florida

Printed and bound in Singapore

ABOUT THIS BOOK

This is one of a set of 10 books that tells the story of the Renaissance—a time of discovery and change in the world. It was during this period—roughly from 1375 to 1575—that adventurous mariners from Europe sailed the vast oceans in tiny ships and found the Americas and new sea routes to the Spice Islands of the East. The influx of gold and silver from the New World and the increase in trade made many merchants and traders in Europe extremely rich. They spent some of their wealth on luxury goods like paintings and gold and silver items for their homes, and this created a new demand for the work of artists of all kinds. Europe experienced a cultural flowering as great artists like Leonardo da Vinci, Michelangelo, and Raphael produced masterpieces that have never been surpassed.

At the same time, scholars were rediscovering the works of the ancient Greek and Roman writers, and this led to a new way of looking at the world based on observation and the importance of the individual. This humanism, together with other new ideas, spread more rapidly than ever before thanks to the development of printing with movable type.

There was upheaval in the church too. Thinkers such as Erasmus and Luther began to question the teachings of the established church, and this eventually led to a breakaway from the Catholic church and the setting up of Protestant churches—an event called the Reformation.

The set focuses on Europe, but it also looks at how societies in other parts of the world such as Africa, China, India, and the Americas were developing, and the ways in which the Islamic and Christian worlds interacted.

The entries in this set are arranged alphabetically and are illustrated with paintings, photographs, drawings, and maps, many from the Renaissance period. Each entry ends with a list of cross-references to other entries in the set, and at the end of each book there is a timeline to help you relate events to one another in time.

There is also a useful "Further Reading" list that includes websites, a glossary of special terms, and an index covering the whole set.

Contents

VOLUME 7

Michelangelo

In his lifetime Michelangelo (1475–1564) was recognized as a genius—many called him "the divine Michelangelo"—and he is still one of the most famous artists ever to have lived. He excelled at painting, sculpture, and architecture, and brought an unrivaled power and dynamism to the portrayal of the human form. He produced some of the best-known works of art in the Western world, including his sculpture of the Old Testament hero David and his paintings on the ceiling of the Sistine Chapel in Rome.

Michelangelo Buonarroti was born on March 6, 1475, in the village of Caprese in the hills above the city of Florence in northern Italy. His father came from a good family but had little money. At first he opposed his son's wish to become an artist, which was still considered a fairly lowly occupation, but eventually he relented. At the age of 13 Michelangelo became an apprentice in the studio of Domenico Ghirlandaio, a popular Florentine painter.

Michelangelo never completed his apprenticeship. At the age of 14 he carved a statue that attracted the notice

Above: This scene from Michelangelo's paintings on the Sistine Chapel ceiling (1508–1512) shows God creating Adam. Encircled by a billowing cloak and supported by angels, God stretches forward and imparts the energy of life to his adoring creation.

of Lorenzo the Magnificent, head of the Medici, who were the most powerful family in Florence and great patrons of the arts. He invited Michelangelo to live in his palace, where he was educated with Lorenzo's own son Giovanni and his nephew Giulio. There Michelangelo also studied sculpture under the guidance of the artist Bertoldo di Giovanni, who looked after the Medici collection of art, which included many pieces of classical (ancient Greek and Roman) sculpture.

Michelangelo was deeply influenced by classical sculpture throughout his life. One of his earliest surviving works is a relief sculpture (a sculpture carved on a flat background) that was inspired by carvings from Roman sarcophaguses (stone coffins). It shows a battle scene in which nude (unclothed)

Below: The Pietà *(1498–1500) by Michelangelo. Michelangelo interpreted the subject of Mary with the dead Christ in a new way, creating a quiet, serene sculpture that encourages reflection on Christ's sacrifice for humankind.*

figures twist in violent movement, another theme that appears throughout his work.

In 1492 Lorenzo de Medici died suddenly. A short while after, northern Italy was invaded by French troops, and the Medici were ousted from power. At the age of 19 Michelangelo left Florence in search of new patrons and work. He traveled to the neighboring city of Bologna, where he carved several small statues for the church of San Domenico, and then went on to Rome. There, for a wealthy banker he carved a life-size statue of Bacchus, the ancient Roman god of wine. He combined a lifelike portrayal of the young god's solid body, influenced by Roman sculpture, with a sophisticated pose conveying his drunkenness.

EARLY FAME

In 1498–1500 Michelangelo carved his first major work, a colossal statue for the tomb of a French cardinal. It is a pietà, which means "pity" in Italian and is the name given to works of art that show the Virgin Mary with the body of the crucified Christ. This subject was popular in northern Europe, but most versions were rather grisly. In contrast, Michelangelo's statue is serene and beautiful, letting the tragedy of Christ's sacrifice unfold through his limp body that lies across Mary's lap and through her sad, downward gaze. The *Pietà* won Michelangelo great fame at the age of just 24.

In 1501 Michelangelo returned to Florence. There the cathedral governors appointed him to carve a huge block of marble over 16 ft (5m) high. Another sculptor had started carving the block 40 years earlier, but

Below: The sculpture of David (1501–1504) by Michelangelo, showing him as a strong young man.

had abandoned the project. Michelangelo decided to carve a huge statue of the Old Testament hero David, who killed the giant Goliath.

Michelangelo spent three years sculpting *David*, finishing in 1504. The result was acclaimed by the citizens of Florence, and it remains one of the best-known sculptures in Western art. Michelangelo portrayed David as a strong, handsome youth with a watchful expression on his face, as if readying himself for battle with Goliath. The Florentines saw the statue as a symbol of their own city, proudly holding its own among larger Italian states.

BATTLE SCENES

Following the triumph of *David*, the governors of Florence asked Michelangelo to paint a large fresco (a painting made on wet plaster) on a wall of the council chamber, depicting one of the city-state's military victories. Fellow artist Leonardo da Vinci was engaged to paint another battle scene on the opposite wall. Michelangelo made many studies and a full-size cartoon (drawing) for his picture, *The Battle of Cascina*, which was filled with nude human figures twisting and writhing as they fought. He probably never started the painting, but the drawings were much admired and copied by later artists.

By now Michelangelo was in great demand as an artist. Fired by a desire to create works on a grand scale, he took on a series of jobs too huge for even

him to complete—a habit that was to plague him for the rest of his life. In 1505 he was summoned to Rome by Pope Julius II, who asked him to carve him a tomb involving 40 large marble statues. Even with Michelangelo's energy this project was impossible for one man to complete. It hung over him like a cloud for the next 40 years.

Michelangelo spent the next eight months at the famous marble quarries in Carrara, northern Italy, selecting

---

Fired by a desire to create works on a grand scale, Michelangelo took on a series of jobs too huge for even him to complete

---

blocks of stone for the project. However, in 1505 Julius gave him a new task: to paint the ceiling of the Sistine Chapel in the Vatican Palace in Rome. The chapel had been built by Pope Sixtus IV in the 1470s, and other artists had already decorated the walls when Julius asked Michelangelo to paint the ceiling. Michelangelo was reluctant to take on the project, arguing that he was a sculptor, not a painter, but the pope was determined. Michelangelo began work in 1508 and finished four years later in 1512. His frescoes met with immediate acclaim, and the Sistine Chapel ceiling remains his most famous work.

Pope Julius died just four months later. The new pope, Leo X, was Giovanni de Medici, whom Michelangelo had known as a boy. Pope Leo urged Michelangelo to start work on Julius's tomb, and he carved two figures of slaves and a huge statue of the

THE CEILING OF THE SISTINE CHAPEL

The Sistine Chapel is part of the Vatican Palace in Rome, where the pope lives, and in the Renaissance was used for important state occasions. When Julius II engaged Michelangelo to decorate the ceiling, he suggested a design with pictures of the 12 apostles. However, Michelangelo proposed a more ambitious scheme with paintings illustrating Old Testament stories. Julius approved, and work began in 1508.

Arranged down the middle of the ceiling are nine large pictures: three showing the creation of the world, three showing the stories of Adam and Eve, and three showing the stories of Noah. Nude male figures flank each picture. Around the edge of the ceiling Michelangelo painted 12 large figures of prophets and sibyls (female prophets) who foretold Christ's birth and below them pictures of Christ's ancestors, starting with Abraham.

The gently curving ceiling is about the size of a tennis court and at its highest point rises 65 ft (20m) above the chapel floor. The task of painting it was colossal. Michelangelo lay on wooden scaffolding and painted all day long. He worked alone, dismissing assistants because their work was not good enough. He painted with great assurance, often applying the paint directly without drawing out the design on the ceiling first as most artists would have done. Working in this way, he successfully translated the powerful, expressive style he had developed in his sculptures to the painted ceiling. By October 1512 the enormous and complex project was complete.

Right: The Sistine Chapel, with Michelangelo's ceiling painted with scenes from the Old Testament.

prophet Moses—another powerful, muscular figure. Later, the project was scaled down so it involved fewer figures, but it still dragged on for years.

NEW ASSIGNMENTS

Michelangelo spent the period 1516–1534 back in Florence, mainly working for the Medici, who had regained control of the city. The family gave him another daunting task: to design a chapel with marble tombs for four Medici princes, including Lorenzo the Magnificent. He started work; but in the late 1520s the Medici were again ousted from power in Florence, and a new republican government took control. In the service of the new regime Michelangelo worked as an architect, designing fortifications for the city. When the Medici reconquered Florence in 1530, Michelangelo fled from his former masters in fear of his life. But the pope sent word he would not be punished if he resumed work on the Medici chapel. He eventually completed two out of the four tombs.

THE LAST JUDGMENT

In 1534, in his late 50s, Michelangelo left Florence for good, returning to Rome to work for another pope, Paul III. Now his job was to paint another huge fresco in the Sistine Chapel, this time for the wall behind the altar. Michelangelo covered the whole area with a picture of the Last Judgment, when Christians believe that Christ will come to earth a second time and judge the souls of the dead, sending them to heaven or hell. Michelangelo used somber colors, mainly browns for the human figures and blue for the sky, and a looser style. The painting is very different from the spirit of his earlier works and is filled with pain and menace. It took him seven years to complete and as usual was greatly admired when it was unveiled. However, some people criticized the

Left: **The Last Judgment (1534–1541) by Michelangelo. Christ is shown in the center of the painting with his right arm raised to condemn the damned. The swirling mass of figures around him includes the damned falling to hell (bottom right) and the blessed rising to heaven (bottom left). Michelangelo also included a self-portrait in the painting, in the face of the flayed skin of Saint Bartholomew, which is held by the muscular male figure below Christ to the right.**

MICHELANGELO'S ARCHITECTURE

Michelangelo brought the same power and dynamism that characterize his sculpture and painting to his designs for buildings. Architecture gave him the opportunity to explore the interplay of forms and space on a much larger scale. His earliest architectural work was for the Medici family and included a chapel and a library annex at the church of San Lorenzo in Florence, both designed in the 1520s. He used features of classical architecture, like columns, but in a new, more sculptural way, sometimes disregarding the rules that other Renaissance architects had worked out, and his work is often regarded as "mannerist." In the 1540s Pope Paul III engaged Michelangelo to work on two building projects that were a central part of the papacy's plans to rebuild Rome as a great and powerful city. The first involved remodeling the Capitoline Hill, the center of the secular (nonreligious) city government. Michelangelo gave the government buildings on the Capitoline imposing fronts with giant columns and designed a pavement with an unusual oval pattern in the piazza (square) around which they stood. The second project was the new Saint Peter's basilica (church). Although other architects worked on the building, and Michelangelo died before it was completed, his design shaped the appearance of Saint Peter's, particularly its great dome.

Above: The staircase and entrance hall designed by Michelangelo for the Laurentian Library, which is attached to the church of San Lorenzo in Florence.

inclusion of so many nude figures, which they felt were inappropriate for a religious painting, particularly on an altar wall. After Michelangelo's death draperies (clothes) were painted over many of the nudes.

LATE WORK

Michelangelo continued to work in his 70s and 80s, though mainly as an architect. He designed the great dome of Saint Peter's in the Vatican and personally oversaw its construction. He also painted two more large frescoes in the Vatican, *The Conversion of Saint Paul* and *The Crucifixion of Saint Peter*, and continued to sculpt, carving two more pietàs. He was still working on one of them just a week before he died, on February 18, 1564, at the age of 89.

After being honored in Rome, Michelangelo's body was buried in his native city of Florence. Both in life and death he exerted an enormous influence on art that has continued to the present day. In the 16th century his virtuosity (great skill) and expressive treatment of the human form influenced mannerist artists, while in the 17th century the power and drama of his style influenced baroque artists. His originality, independent spirit, and success shaped modern ideas of the artist as a creative genius. The Italian art historian Giorgio Vasari called him "the greatest man known to the arts."

Miniatures

In art the term "miniature" is used to describe two sorts of picture: paintings decorating illuminated (illustrated) manuscripts and small paintings, especially portraits, that can be held in the hand or worn as jewelry. While manuscript illumination flourished in the Middle Ages, portrait miniatures first became popular in the 16th century at the French and English royal courts.

Even after the invention of printing in the 15th century wealthy people continued to have their books illustrated and decorated with small, brilliantly colored paintings. Many painters and workshops specialized in these miniature illustrations, and the tradition was particularly strong in Flanders, in cities such as Ghent and Bruges.

ROOTS OF THE TRADITION

The portrait miniature emerged from this tradition of manuscript painting in northern Europe and also from the fashion for medals in Italy. Medals had become popular from the 1430s, when they were used to commemorate powerful men and women and their achievements. Medals had lifelike portraits on the front, usually in profile (showing a side view of the face), and were often round or oval. They were given to loyal courtiers and were visible signs of their allegiance.

Above: A portrait miniature (about 1540) by Holbein showing Jane Pemberton, the wife of a London merchant. It has a precious setting with pearls and would have been worn as jewelry.

Early portrait miniatures were similar in size, shape, and function to medals. They were painted in watercolor on vellum, a fine parchment made from the skin of young animals, although later artists also used oil paint with ivory and wood as backgrounds. Miniatures were worn as jewelry in lockets around the neck, chest, or upper arm, or were kept in small boxes. Like medals, miniatures often showed just the head and shoulders of the person portrayed, although many depicted the sitter full length (showing their whole body). Courtiers were expected to own a miniature of their king or queen; but miniatures also had a more intimate use: to remind people of their loved ones, much as photographs do today.

THE FIRST PORTRAIT MINIATURES

Scholars think that the first miniature portraits were made in France. The earliest mention of them dates from 1526, when Marguerite of Navarre, the sister of King Francis II of France, sent King Henry VIII of England two lockets whose lids could be opened to reveal portraits—one showed Francis and the other his two sons. These lockets no longer exist, although a a few by Jean Clouet, another court artist working for Francis II, have survived.

At about the same time, the Flemish-born artist Lucas Horenbout (about 1490–1544) began producing miniatures at Henry VIII's court in England. Horenbout began an important tradition of miniature painting in England, which became the main home of the art form. His

England became the main home of miniature painting

immediate successor was the German artist Hans Holbein (1497–1543), who was Henry VIII's favorite court painter. Although Holbein is best-known for his full-size portraits, he also painted a number of miniatures, 12 of which survive. They are all painted in the same clear, imposing style he used for his full-size pictures, with precise outlines and smooth brushwork.

ELIZABETHAN MINIATURES

However, the great age of miniature painting in England came in the late 16th century and early 17th century, particularly in the work of Nicholas Hilliard (about 1547–1619) and Isaac Oliver (about 1556–1617). Both men worked at the court of Queen Elizabeth I and developed delicate, decorative styles that perfectly capture the elegant fashions of the Elizabethan era. Their sons continued the tradition, and portrait miniatures remained popular until the 19th century, when they were superseded by photographs.

NICHOLAS HILLIARD

Nicholas Hilliard is the most famous and admired of all English miniaturists. He was also a goldsmith and jeweler, and from about 1570 worked for Queen Elizabeth I of England. In about 1600 he wrote a treatise (book) called *The Arte of Limning* ("limning" is an old word for miniature portraiture), which gives an account of his working methods. Hilliard painted miniatures of the queen and her leading courtiers, including Francis Drake, Walter Raleigh, and Philip Sidney. However, his best-known work shows an unidentified young man in splendid clothes leaning against a tree. It is a decorative, elegant picture that reflects the ardor and intimacy found in the love sonnets of Elizabethan poets.

Right: Hilliard's best-known miniature, **Young Man among Roses** *(about 1587). It is painted in watercolor on vellum.*

SEE ALSO

♦ Elizabeth I
♦ Holbein
♦ Marguerite of Navarre
♦ Medals and Coins
♦ Portraiture

Mining

Precious and base metals were in great demand in the Renaissance. Gold and silver were used to make coins and jewelry, iron was used for armor, and copper was needed to make bronze cannon. All these metals, together with lead and tin, had to be dug out of the ground, or mined. Coal for fuel and salt for preserving and flavoring food were also mined.

There were two main methods of mining in the Middle Ages. One was called "open pit." The miners dug a large pit and then hacked out the ore (rocks from which the metal was extracted) using hand tools like hammers and picks. Another method was to dig tunnels to reach deposits further underground. The tunnels were dangerous and often collapsed. They also filled up with water when they went too deep, so channels had to be dug to drain the water away.

By the 14th and early 15th centuries mining output had declined as surface ores were exhausted. Rich deposits still existed deeper underground, but could not be reached because water flooded the mines. However, new developments in technology helped miners overcome these problems.

One new development was the suction pump, which was used to drain the mines of water. The pumps were driven by water mills, which had other uses as well. A mill could drive a set of bellows to increase the temperature in

Left: A detail from a 16th-century French painting of a copper mine. Mounds of metallic ore can be seen in the foreground, while in the background miners tend the furnace that separates the copper from the ore.

the furnace used to separate the metals from their ores. Water mills could also drive hammers and saws—hammers pounded lumps of hot metal into shape, while saws cut timber into pieces of wood that could be used to prop up mine shafts. Water mills were expensive to build, however.

The techniques used to separate metals from their ores were also costly. For example, lead was needed to separate silver from copper ore. The richest deposits of lead in central Europe were found in the South Tyrol region of Austria, while the most extensive silver reserves were located in the North Tyrol region on the other side of the Alps. Getting the lead from one region to the other over the mountains was an expensive business.

NEED FOR INVESTMENT

The mining industry needed a huge amount of investment. At the end of the 15th century the price of metals rose high enough to attract investment from businessmen, most of whom were merchants who had accumulated fortunes in trade. These merchants bought the rights to mine for metals from the noblemen who owned the land on which the mines were located. To do so, they often raised additional funds from investors not directly involved in mining.

The most profitable metals were silver and copper. While iron ore was scattered across the face of Europe, the richest deposits of silver and copper were concentrated in specific areas. The most important were Thuringia in present-day Germany, the North Tyrol, and Slovakia, then a part of Hungary. This concentration allowed certain mining companies to dominate their supply. For example, from the late 15th century the German Fugger family had

Left: An illustration from a 16th-century German book on mining, showing a machine used for washing the ore after it had been brought up out of the ground.

complete control over the supply of copper and silver from Hungary.

The European discovery of the Americas at the end of the 15th century presented new mining opportunities. In 1545 huge deposits of silver were discovered in the Andes Mountains. Some of these veins of ore had a pure silver content of 50 percent, compared with only 1 percent in Europe. Between 1550 and 1580 these new sources were exploited by the forced labor of local people who extracted the ores with primitive equipment.

The decline of the native population through disease meant that the mining companies had to introduce more advanced techniques, similar to those used in Europe. They were expensive to implement because of the extremely high altitudes at which the Andean mines were located. However, even though the initial costs were great, the rewards for investors were enormous.

SEE ALSO

♦ Americas
♦ Bankers and Banking
♦ Exploration
♦ Medals and Coins
♦ Merchants
♦ Technology
♦ Trade

Left: A 16th-century painting showing a Dominican missionary baptizing Native American converts in Mexico, watched by Spanish soldiers.

Missionaries

The Renaissance saw a great expansion of Christianity throughout the world. As Europeans explored and settled in new lands, they sought to convert the native people to their own religion. Missionaries traveled immense distances, driven by religious zeal to convert pagan peoples to Christianity. The most successful missionaries were Roman Catholic, who preached the Christian message everywhere from Peru to Japan. In the 16th century Protestant lands had less contact with non-Christians, and Protestant leaders were not so concerned to spread Christianity beyond Europe.

Three large Catholic empires were responsible for most missionary work—those of Spain, Portugal, and France. As a result Christianity was soon firmly established in the Americas and the Philippines. Jesuit missionaries also set up missions in India, Japan, and China.

MISSIONARY ZEAL

Today it is difficult to understand the urgency the missionaries brought to their work. Some of them, especially the Franciscans, believed that Christ would return when all the peoples of the world had converted to Christianity. Missionaries in Mexico reported baptizing 1,500 converts a day. Some resorted to bizarre methods to impress the native people, including one (failed) attempt to walk on water.

Most missionaries were selected from the religious orders of the Augustinians, Dominicans, and Franciscans and, from 1542, the Jesuits. Competition for a mission post could be intense. One applicant applied 21 times in 32 years, while another showed his enthusiasm by writing the pope a letter in his own blood.

ACROSS THE WORLD

The Catholic mission spread rapidly across the newly discovered world. The earliest Renaissance missions centered on Africa and had great success with King Nzina Nkuwu of the Congo, who converted and changed his name to John in 1491. Franciscan missionaries accompanied the Portuguese explorer Pedro Álvares Cabral in 1500 on the voyage that led to the discovery of Brazil and brought the Portuguese to India for the second time.

One of the earliest missionaries in the Americas was the Dominican Bartolomé de las Casas, who arrived in Hispaniola in 1502. He worked tirelessly to improve the conditions of the Native Americans and campaigned against their slavery. The first missionaries arrived in Mexico in 1524, and Mexico then became a base for missions across the Pacific to the Philippines, beginning around 1565.

In the New World missionaries built many mission churches. As well as converting the local people to Christianity, they also tried to educate them and improve their living conditions. In South America the Jesuits established Christian villages where they taught the inhabitants trades and tried to protect them from

the Europeans, who wanted them to work on the sugar plantations, where they were cruelly exploited and treated as little better than slaves.

MANY ROLES

The missionaries contributed to local life in a variety of ways. In the New World they improved agriculture by introducing new crops and animals. In China a Jesuit missionary served as astronomer in the imperial court. Missionaries were prepared to turn their hand to almost anything, working as teachers, doctors, architects, cooks, or diplomats. Despite all this work, they often suffered under a brutal boredom. One Jesuit in California broke the monotony by keeping track of how many scorpions he killed (500 in 13 years).

THE LANGUAGE BARRIER

The greatest difficulty to overcome was the language barrier. To make his point one missionary in North America taught the concept of hell by setting fire to a village's livestock. However, most missionaries mastered the local language, and the first dictionaries and grammar books for many native languages were composed by missionaries.

Above: An example of picture writing developed by missionaries in Latin America to help them communicate with Native Americans who could not speak Spanish.

SEE ALSO

♦ Africa
♦ Americas
♦ Biblical Studies
♦ Catholic Church
♦ China
♦ Counter Reformation
♦ Exploration
♦ Japan
♦ Jesuits
♦ Religious Orders

Monteverdi

The composer Claudio Monteverdi (1567–1643) was born in Cremona in northern Italy. As a young man he studied at the city's cathedral with Marcantonio Ingegneri, a well-known local musician. Monteverdi's first music was published while he was still a teenager. Around 1591 he moved to the court of Duke Vincenzo Gonzaga in Mantua, where he was employed as a string player and later as a composer.

At this time a new art form, opera, was beginning to develop. Operas are dramatic performances in which the words are sung. In the late 16th century a group of composers and poets in Florence composed the first simple pieces of the type. Their work influenced Monteverdi, who composed his own opera, *Orfeo*, in 1607.

The work, which retold the ancient Greek myth of Orpheus and Eurydice, proved to be a huge step forward from earlier operas. Monteverdi tried to bring out the drama in the storyline by matching the mood of the action with that of the music, a revolutionary approach. *Orfeo* is still regularly performed today and is now seen as the first great opera.

SAINT MARK'S

Despite his success, Monteverdi was dismissed from his post when the duke of Mantua died in 1612. Almost immediately he was offered the highly prestigious job of director of music at the church of Saint Mark's in Venice. He was to hold the position until his

death in 1643. During this period he wrote a great deal of music for the church, such as masses and psalms.

In the last years of his life Monteverdi turned toward opera again. In 1637 the first public opera house opened in Venice, and Monteverdi wrote several works for it. All but three of Monteverdi's operas have now been lost, the surviving works being *Orfeo*, *The Coronation of Poppea*, and *The Return of Ulysses to His Country*. However, Monteverdi is still seen as one of the most influential composers in the history of opera.

Above: A contemporary portrait of the composer Claudio Monteverdi.

SEE ALSO

♦ Gonzaga Family
♦ Music
♦ Venice

Monuments and Tombs

Some of the greatest works of Renaissance art were monuments and tombs. A monument is a statue or other structure made to commemorate a notable person or event. A particular type of monument is a tomb—a place in which a body is buried or a memorial placed over the grave or nearby.

The rulers of Italy's city-states commissioned monuments to show pride in their city. Many of the monuments built in Renaissance Florence echoed the styles of classical Roman sculpture, reflecting Florence's claim to be strong and independent like ancient Rome. One type of classical monument that was popular was the equestrian monument, which showed a figure on horseback and celebrated military excellence. Several of them showed the horse with one leg raised from the ground—testing the sculptor's skill to make the monument stay upright. Two famous equestrian monuments are by Donatello and Andrea del Verrocchio. Donatello's *Gattamelata* monument in Padua (1445–1453) and Verrocchio's *Colleoni* monument, completed in 1496 in Venice, both commemorate soldiers.

MEMORIALS TO WEALTHY PEOPLE

The growing power of princely rulers in Renaissance Italy meant that monuments were increasingly built to celebrate individuals, and many imposing tombs were commissioned by wealthy patrons. In Italy a favorite type of tomb was the wall tomb, in which a sculpted figure of the person commemorated was set in a framework of architectural elements (columns or arches) placed against an interior wall of a church or chapel. Sometimes the tomb included an effigy, which was an image of the deceased person. Often, there were other figures as well, usually representing saints or angels.

THE MEDICI TOMBS

Probably the best-known examples of wall tombs are the pair made by Michelangelo for Giuliano and Lorenzo de Medici in the family chapel in the church of San Lorenzo, Florence. Michelangelo worked on these wall

Above: The marble wall tomb made by Michelangelo for Giuliano, duke of Nemours, one of the powerful Medici family of Florence. Michelangelo was also commissioned to build a matching tomb for Lorenzo de Medici—neither tomb was ever completely finished.

Left: The tomb of Henry VII of England and his wife Elizabeth of York, which was designed by the Italian sculptor Pietro Torrigiani. While the bronze figures are similar to earlier Gothic effigies, the ornate details around the tomb edge show the influence of Italian Renaissance style.

tombs on and off during the 1520s and 1530s. He also spent 40 years (1505–1545) working from time to time on another tomb, for Pope Julius II. It was intended to be the largest and grandest tomb of the age—almost a building in itself and adorned with about 40 life-size statues. After the pope died in 1513, the project was drastically reduced in scale, and a much smaller tomb was produced (mainly carved by assistants). It does, however, feature one of Michelangelo's most famous statues—the majestic seated figure of Moses. The tomb is in the church of San Pietro in Rome.

BEYOND ITALY

Many prominent people outside Italy also commissioned imposing tombs during the Renaissance. One of the most important tombs in England was made by Pietro Torrigiano (1472–1528). Torrigiano had studied with Michelangelo (and broken his nose when they got into a fight). Torrigiano spent about a decade in England, where in 1512–1518 he made the tomb of King Henry VII and his wife Elizabeth of York for Westminster Abbey in London. It is of a type called a tomb-chest in which the figures lie on a chestlike block of stone. Torrigiano's elegant bronze figures of the king and queen show the influence of the English tradition of Gothic art, but in the ornamental detail he used Renaissance motifs. This tomb marked the first time pure Italian features had appeared in England.

In France there was a fashion for tombs depicting a realistic corpse, sometimes showing the stitches where the body had been sewn up after embalming or even representing the body in a state of decomposition. On some French tombs the deceased person is portrayed twice, on two levels; below, he or she is shown lying dead, and above, he or she is shown alive, praying. One example of this type, in the Abbey Church of Saint Denis near Paris (the royal burial church), is the tomb of King Henry II and his wife Catherine de Medici (begun 1561). The tomb was designed by the Italian artist Francesco Primaticcio (1505–1570), and the figures are by Germain Pilon (1525–1590), a great French sculptor.

SEE ALSO

♦ Donatello
♦ Gothic Art
♦ Julius II
♦ Medici Family
♦ Michelangelo
♦ Sculptors' Materials and Techniques
♦ Sculpture

More, Thomas

Sir Thomas More (1477–1535) was both a celebrated scholar and a gifted administrator who rose to the high office of lord chancellor of England. Because of his strong Catholic faith he refused to recognize King Henry VIII as supreme head of the Church of England; his refusal ultimately led to his execution.

Left: This portrait shows Thomas More as a young man. A highly talented lawyer and administrator, More rose to become one of the most important political figures in England.

More was a brilliant student, and he excelled at both his school and the University of Oxford. In 1496 he was admitted to Lincoln's Inn, where he trained to become a lawyer. During his time there More lived in a nearby monastery. He was an extremely pious man and for a long time considered becoming a priest. Ultimately, however, he decided that the religious life was not for him. Nevertheless, he remained deeply committed to his faith for the rest of his life.

While working as a lawyer, More demonstrated considerable diplomatic skills, negotiating on behalf of several London companies in trade disputes with foreign merchants. His talents brought him to the attention of Henry VIII, and from around 1521 onward he became the king's right-hand man, acting as an adviser, secretary, and confidant. He welcomed foreign emissaries, drafted the king's speeches, and read his private correspondence.

LITERARY WORKS

At the same time, More published a series of books on philosophy, establishing a reputation as one of the foremost humanist scholars of Europe.

Like his friend Erasmus, he placed a great value on the study of ancient Greek and Latin texts. More's most famous literary work, *Utopia*, presented an ideal city-state. In the book he discussed a wide range of matters, from state education and women's rights to divorce and euthanasia (mercy killing).

In 1529 More succeeded Cardinal Wolsey as lord chancellor. The king had already sought More's advice about his plans to divorce his first wife, Catherine of Aragon, and marry Anne Boleyn. More believed that Catherine was the king's true, legal wife, and in 1530 he refused to sign a letter asking the pope to annul the marriage. He also refused to attend the coronation of Anne Boleyn in 1533 or recognize Henry as the head of the Church of England. He was arrested for treason in the following year. Found guilty, he was beheaded on July 6, 1535.

SEE ALSO

♦ Erasmus
♦ Henry VIII
♦ Humanism
♦ Utopias

Music

Like painting and sculpture, music thrived in the Renaissance. Musicians and composers were employed both at royal courts and by the church. The music that they wrote could thus be either religious or secular (nonreligious) in content. The period saw the development of older musical forms such as the motet, the mass, and the chanson, as well as the birth of new musical form—opera.

At the beginning of the Renaissance period one of the most popular forms of music was a type of song known as the motet. The first motets were

Left: Singers accompanied by a lute player, shown in a 15th-century painting called A Concert, *by Lorenzo Costa (1459–1535). The lute was a popular instrument for accompanying songs in the 15th century and was later to become an important solo instrument.*

written in France in the early 13th century. They were usually based around earlier plainsong (single-line) melodies and were polyphonic in style. Polyphonic music uses many different voices, all of them equally important. In a motet the lowest voice—called the tenor—sang the original plainsong melody in Latin. The other voices sang new melodies over the top of it. The words to these new parts were usually French. Motets could have either religious or secular themes.

The style of motet writing varied from composer to composer. Some composers wrote for one or more choirs instead of solo singers. Others used both choir and soloists. Eventually, instruments began to play an important accompanying part, as well as introducing variety through instrumental interludes. Motet music almost always used imitation, with one voice echoing the words or music of another. One of the most important composers of motets was Orlando di Lasso (about 1532–1594), who wrote more than 500 examples of the style.

THE MASS

Another important form of music in the Renaissance period was the mass. The mass is a church ritual that consists of five sections—the Kyrie, Gloria, Credo, Sanctus, and Benedictus. The chants that made up the ritual had been put to music for several centuries, but in the 16th century this music became more complex. Two of the greatest composers of the mass at this time were Josquin Desprez (about 1440–1521) and Giovanni Pierluigi da Palestrina (about 1525–1594). About 20 of the masses Josquin wrote survive today as well as over 100 of Palestrina's.

Choral music was extremely important in the Renaissance, and by the 15th

PLAINSONG

Plainsong (or "plainchant") is the earliest known church music. It is distinguished by its slow and extremely simple single-line melodies, which were sung by voices in unison. Much of plainsong dates back to the time of Pope Gregory I (about 540–604), who arranged for many of the chants to be written down and categorized. Because of Gregory's work plainsong is also known as Gregorian chant.

The words of plainsong were always in Latin. For the first 1,000 years of its existence the church would not allow instruments to perform at its services because they were associated with worldly pleasures such as dancing. For this reason plainsong melodies were originally sung unaccompanied. Plainsong is still performed today.

Above: An illustration from a 15th-century English manuscript showing a choir of monks singing plainsong.

century many churches had their own training schools for choirs. The churches often served as influential centers of music. One of the most famous of them was the cathedral of Saint Mark's in Venice. It employed two choirs, which were located on opposite sides of the building. The cathedral's director of music, Adrian Willaert (1490–1562), wrote pieces that were

Left: A 16th-century book illustration showing the French poet and composer Guillaume de Machaut receiving a visit from Nature (wearing a crown), who presents to him her three children, Emotion, Rhetoric, and Music. Machaut was one of the first composers to write chansons, an important form of secular music in the Renaissance.

specifically designed to take advantage of this unusual arrangement.

Renaissance church choirs were entirely male. Women were only allowed to sing in services as members of the congregation. The upper vocal parts were sung by men using the highest range of their voice—the falsetto register. The falsetto register is not normally used and sounds slightly unnatural. It is not nearly as strong as a woman's natural singing voice, which was already being used in secular music by the mid-16th century.

This need for stronger voices to sing the upper parts led to the creation of a new voice—that of the castrato, or male soprano. However, the voice could only be obtained through ex-treme measures—by castrating a boy before puberty, enabling his high, unchanged voice to persist into manhood. Although this practice was never seen as acceptable in northern Europe, castratos continued to perform in Italy until the 19th century.

SECULAR MUSIC

Not all music written in the Renaissance period was produced for the church. Many musicians and composers were employed at royal courts, where they produced both religious and secular music. One of the main forms of secular music in the Renaissance period was the chanson (French for "song"). Unlike earlier nonreligious songs, chansons were polyphonic. The lyrics to chansons told of love and chivalry. The first major composer to experiment in this style was Guillaume de Machaut (about 1300–1377). The chanson was later developed by composers such as

Guillaume Dufay (about 1398–1474) and Gilles de Bins dit Binchois (about 1400–1460).

In Italy the term "madrigal" was used for a similar light-hearted composition for two or three voices. However, by about 1530 the madrigal had developed into a much more serious work. It used great works of poetry as its inspiration, and much importance was placed on "word painting"—illustrating the meaning of the words through the music. Words such as "dropping" or "falling" were always set to a descending melody, while dissonances (clashing notes) were used on words of suffering, such as "pain." A book of translated Italian madrigals called *Musica Transalpina* ("Music from Across the Alps") brought the madrigal to England. There it enjoyed enormous popularity thanks to the work of composers like Thomas Morley (1557–1602).

LOOKING BACKWARD

Toward the end of the 16th century a number of composers began to look back to ancient Greece and Rome for their inspiration. They were following in the footsteps of Renaissance artists and sculptors, who were able to see and copy a great number of surviving artworks from the Greek and Roman periods. However, composers had no ancient pieces of music to study or admire. Although the Greeks and Romans placed great importance on music, they had no way of writing it down. What had survived instead from these ancient times was a wealth of theoretical writings about music.

To the Greeks and Romans the purest form of music was a single melodic line—a monody. A number of composers saw that this idea had possibilities for their own music.

Among them was a group of artists and musicians who met in Florence, Italy, and who became known as the Florentine Camerata. One of the group, the composer Jacopo Peri (1561–1633), began experimenting with setting words to single-line melodies in a new way so that the natural rhythm of the spoken words was mirrored in the music. This new style of combining words and music marked the beginning of opera. This new musical form developed rapidly in the early years of the 17th century, particularly through the work of Claudio Monteverdi (1567–1643).

Below: The title page of the counter-tenor's part for **Psalmes, Sonets, and Songes of Sadnes and Pietie** *by the English composer William Byrd. Byrd wrote many songs as well as a great deal of instrumental music.*

CONTRATENOR.
Pſalmes, Sonets, & ſongs of ſadnes and pietie, made into Muſicke of fiue parts : whereof, ſome of them going abroad among diuers, in vntrue coppies, are heere truely corrected, and th'other being Songs very rare & newly compoſed, are heere publiſhed, for the recreation of all ſuch as delight in Muſick: By *William Byrd,* one of the Gent. of the Queenes Maieſtie; honorable Chappell.

Printed by Thomas Eaſt, the aſſigne of VV. Byrd, and are to be ſold at the dweiling houſe of the ſaid T. Eaſt, by Paules wharfe. 1588.
Cum priuilegio Regiæ Maieſtatis.

MUSIC APPEARS IN PRINT

Printing developed in Germany in the middle of the 15th century, and by the 1470s music was also being printed. The first printed music books were published in Rome in 1476 and were of plainsong. The first books of polyphonic music were not published until 1501, by the Italian printer Ottaviano dei Petrucci.

Printing music was a far more complex operation than printing words. The music was first carved onto a wooden block, which was then inked. Red ink was used for the stave lines and black ink for the notes. Each page was printed twice—the staves first, and then the notes. The pages of printed music were then decorated by hand.

Music printing replaced the costly method of copying music by hand, which was a time-consuming task. By the late 15th century many printed copies of music were in circulation, and printers had sprung up all over Europe.

Above: An example of early printed music, dating from 1512.

Interest in instrumental music grew rapidly in the Renaissance period. Instruments began to play a more important part, moving away from their traditional role of simply giving support to voices. Composers gradually began to add the words "for voices or instruments" on the title pages of their vocal works, while in Germany in 1511 Sebastian Virdung published the first book devoted to musical instruments. Now musicians were able to look up all the technical details they needed to know about tuning, repairing, and maintaining their instruments.

LUTE, VIOL, AND KEYBOARD

Much of the development of instrumental music took place in England. At the end of the 16th century the lute became an important solo instrument thanks to the work of lutenist and composer John Dowland (1563–1626), who wrote over 70 pieces for it. Another important early instrumental composer was William Byrd (1543–1623), who wrote music for the lute and viol (a forerunner of the violin). Byrd also wrote a great deal of keyboard music, though he was greatly exceeded in output by his contemporary John Bull (1562–1628).

Bull was a professional keyboard player, and so it is not surprising that many of his pieces are extremely elaborate, using highly decorated melodies and cascades of running notes. His work looked ahead to the keyboard works of the next 150 years of music history—the baroque era.

SEE ALSO

♦ Drama and Theater
♦ Monteverdi
♦ Musical Instruments
♦ Palestrina

Musical Instruments

Above: This Flemish painting from the mid-16th century shows a man being entertained by two female musicians, one playing the lute and the other the transverse flute.

The musical instruments of the Renaissance, like those that we have today, can be classified into a small number of distinct categories—stringed instruments, keyboard instruments, wind instruments, and percussion.

The most important Renaissance stringed instrument was the lute. It was played like a modern acoustic guitar. The strings were plucked, usually with the fingers, but occasionally with a plectrum. The lute originated in the Arab world and was brought to Europe by the Moors, the Arab conquerors of Spain. It was often used to accompany vocal performances, although it was also played in ensembles and could be used as a solo instrument.

While the lute was plucked, other Renaissance stringed instruments were played with a bow. They were members

---

Viols were forerunners of the modern violin, viola, cello, and double bass

---

of the viol family, the forerunners of the modern violin, viola, cello, and double bass. The viol was rather large and cumbersome, and was played with the lower end of the instrument resting on or between the legs. It had frets (ridges on the fingerboard) like a guitar and was made in many different sizes.

THE VIOLIN

The violin itself was developed in the first half of the 16th century. It was smaller than the viol and had no frets. The violin was descended from a number of different stringed instruments, particularly the *lira da braccio*, which was also played under the chin. Initially, the violin was used for dance music and to accompany singing—it was not seen as a "serious" instrument until the 17th century.

Renaissance musicians also played a wide range of keyboard instruments. One of the most important was the harpsichord, which was often used to accompany vocal performances. The harpsichord had quills that plucked its strings. Two smaller keyboard instruments—the clavichord and the spinet—were used mainly in homes. These instruments were different from the harpsichord in that their strings ran parallel to and diagonally from the keyboard respectively. The strings of the harpsichord ran perpendicular to the keyboard, as in a modern piano. The piano did not appear until the early 18th century. But Renaissance musicians did play another instrument in which, like the piano, the strings were hit rather than plucked—the clavichord.

The oldest keyboard instrument, however, did not use strings at all. The organ produced notes by forcing air through pipes. Organs were usually found in churches and could be huge in size. The 15th-century organ at Amiens cathedral in France boasted a remarkable 2,500 pipes.

WIND INSTRUMENTS

The simplest Renaissance woodwind instrument was the recorder. It was a hollow tube of wood with a mouthpiece and eight holes, which were covered by the fingers and thumb to produce different notes. Recorders came in several sizes, and each size produced notes of a different pitch. In early theater music composers used the recorder to portray pastoral and country scenes and to indicate the presence of supernatural beings.

The sound of the recorder was soft and restrained, similar to that of a close relative—the transverse flute. The flute differed from the recorder in that it was held horizontally. However, unlike its present-day counterpart, it was made from wood rather than metal.

The Renaissance trumpet was very different from the trumpet of today, since it had no valves. In the early Middle Ages it was straight in shape, but in the 15th century it was looped back on itself to make it easier to carry. The trumpet was used at court to perform fanfares to announce the arrival of the sovereign or special guests

The final group of instruments was the percussion family. One popular drum was the tabor, which was small and cylindrical and hung from the player's side. It was hit with a stick rather than the hands. Musicians often used one hand to play the drum and the other to play a small flute. Kettledrums, which were much larger, were introduced into Europe from Central Asia in the 15th century.

Above: This intricately decorated spinet was made in Italy, where the instrument originated. The spinet was much smaller than its close relation the harpsichord.

SEE ALSO

♦ Monteverdi
♦ Music
♦ Palestrina

Mythological Art

Above: The Triumph of Galatea *by Raphael. The nymph Galatea is surrounded by a variety of mythological sea creatures.*

One of the defining features of the Renaissance was the way in which artists looked back to the worlds of ancient Greece and Rome for their inspiration. Of particular interest were the classical world's numerous myths and legends, which provided the subject matter for many of the antique statues and mosaics that influenced Renaissance artists.

By the late 15th century many educated Europeans were becoming increasingly interested in classical texts. The study of Greek and Roman literature was a central part of a new intellectual movement that we know today as humanism. Humanist scholars believed that classical literature offered its readers a fresh way of looking at the world. In keeping with this increased interest in the classical world, artists began to use scenes from Greek and Roman myths as their subject matter.

The myths of the ancient Greeks and Romans were varied in origin. Some of them were connected to historical events, such as those that grew up about the Trojan War. Most of them, however, told stories involving the ancient world's large number of gods and goddesses. After the collapse of the Roman empire in the fifth century A.D. these stories were never entirely forgotten. However, they made almost no appearance in art. The church regarded the classical world as pagan, and for centuries the visual arts were overwhelmingly devoted to Christian subjects.

BOTTICELLI

The first artist to create mythological scenes that were on the same level as major religious works in terms of size and seriousness was Sandro Botticelli (about 1444–1510). Botticelli's first painting to have a classical theme was *Primavera* ("Spring"), completed in about 1477 for the Florentine merchant Lorenzo di Pierfrancesco de Medici. It showed the nymph Chloris being transformed into Flora, the goddess of flowers and spring, by the wind god Zephyr. Botticelli's most famous work, however, was *The Birth of Venus*, an

Left: Parnassus *by Andrea Mantegna. The painting shows the nine goddesses of the arts dancing to the music of the god Apollo, who is playing the lyre. In the center of the painting stand Venus, the Roman goddess of love, and Mars, the god of war.*

elegant painting that depicts the Roman goddess of love being blown to shore on a giant scallop shell. Venus's birth symbolizes the entry of beauty into the world.

By the early 16th century many of the greatest Italian painters had produced notable mythological works, including Leonardo and Raphael in central Italy, Mantegna in Mantua, and Giovanni Bellini, Giorgione, and Titian in Venice. Raphael's *The Triumph of Galatea*, for example, shows the sea-nymph Galatea surrounded by lustful mythological characters. Galatea's gaze is fixed on the figure of Cupid in the top left-hand corner of the painting. Cupid represents the purity of love.

TITIAN

The Venetian painter Titian devoted as much time to mythological works as he did to religious scenes and portraits. His masterpieces include a set of seven scenes based on the Roman poet Ovid's *Metamorphoses* that he painted for

King Philip II of Spain between about 1550 and 1562. The *Metamorphoses* consisted of a series of stories, in each of which a major character was transformed, usually into an animal or a mythical creature. Among the paintings that portray scenes from these stories are *The Rape of Europa*, *Venus and Adonis*, and *Diana and Actaeon*.

In the 16th century mythological art also became well established in countries outside Italy. In Germany, for example, Albrecht Dürer made several engravings of mythological subjects, and Lucas Cranach the Elder produced a series of nudes representing Venus. Mythological subjects were also found in other arts of the time, including tapestry and pottery.

In sculpture small bronzes of mythological figures became particularly popular. The most noted artist producing this kind of work was the Florentine sculptor Giambologna. His most famous work was a bronze statue of the Roman god Mercury.

Naturalism

Above: **The Great Piece of Turf** *(1503) by the German artist Albrecht Dürer. Dürer was one of the first artists to make careful studies of the natural world. This watercolor shows common plants, including grass, dandelions, and plantains.*

The term "naturalism" is used to describe an approach to painting and sculpture in which artists seek to make their work look lifelike, like something that can be seen in the world around us, in "nature." Naturalism is a key theme in Renaissance art and distinguishes it from earlier medieval art that is "stylized," or artificial looking.

Naturalistic art existed in ancient Greek and Roman times long before the Renaissance. Although very few pictures survive from antiquity, written descriptions of paintings have survived that emphasize their lifelike qualities—birds were said to have pecked at a picture of fruit painted by the Greek artist Apelles. Surviving sculptures from ancient Greece and Rome—many of which were known in the Renaissance—also show that naturalism was important in antiquity. Many were portraits or skillful representations of the nude (unclothed) human form. These figure sculptures often went beyond being accurate portrayals of the human body and showed the most beautiful, "idealized" bodies that artists could imagine.

THE MIDDLE AGES

In the Middle Ages artists did not aim to produce lifelike paintings and sculptures. Most art had Christian subjects like God, Christ, Mary, and the saints, and was thought of as showing an otherworldly vision remote from everyday life. The Orthodox Christian church in the Byzantine Empire introduced particularly strict rules for the depiction of holy subjects in images called icons. Icons usually have gold backgrounds, and the holy figure, who is shown looking directly out of the picture, appears flat. The style of Byzantine paintings influenced medieval artists in western Europe; their work, while not bound by such strict rules, is also very stylized. There is no sense that what they depicted is part of everyday life or natural. Artists showed not what they themselves had seen or even imagined but followed a set of traditional images.

From the 13th century in western Europe a few artists began to produce more lifelike sculptures and paintings once again. There are examples of naturalistic carvings and figure sculptures in the new cathedrals that were built in France, Germany, and England at this time. They range from carvings of leaves that are clearly based on the observation of real plants to sculptures of holy figures.

NATURALISM IN ITALIAN ART

The most consistent approach to naturalism emerged in Italian art. In painting one of the first artists to make his pictures look more lifelike was the Florentine painter Giotto (about 1266–1337). In his frescoes (wall paintings made on wet, or "fresh," plaster) he tried to create the impression of solid people situated in three-dimensional spaces such as rooms or landscapes.

He also tried to give them realistic expressions and gestures so that people could identify with them and the story they depicted. However, it was not until the beginning of the 15th century that naturalism became widespread, when artists like Donatello (1386–1466) and Masaccio (1401–1428) were inspired by the ancient Greek and Roman approach to art.

STUDIES FROM NATURE

In order for artists to produce naturalistic paintings and sculptures, they had first to study the world around them. From the 15th century artists began to draw people and objects from life rather than copy existing pictures, as medieval artists had done. Some of the best-known Renaissance drawings were made by Leonardo da Vinci (1452–1519), who produced thousands of studies of the

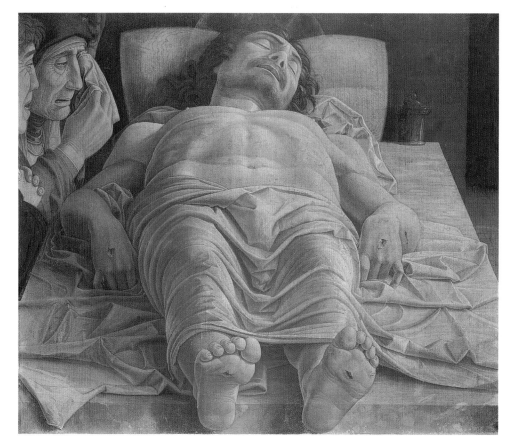

Right: **The Dead Christ** *(about 1480–1490) by the Italian painter Andrea Mantegna. Mantegna painted this powerful picture to show off his knowledge of the human body and perspective. However, he drew Christ's feet smaller and his head larger than they would be in real life so that his unusual interpretation of this holy subject should not appear undignified.*

natural world ranging from plants, animals, and human anatomy to storms and rivers in torrent. The German artist Albrecht Dürer (1471–1528) also made many highly detailed studies to enhance his understanding of the natural world.

"Life drawings," or drawings made by studying a human model, became a central part of artists' training. Following the example of antique art, the human form was regarded as the most noble subject; and since it was also one of the most difficult to portray, it enabled artists to show off their skill.

Sculptors were first to develop the lifelike portrayal of the human figure, drawing directly on their knowledge of antique sculptures and also their study of nature. Donatello's marble statues of saints and Old Testament heroes for the church of Or San Michele and the cathedral in Florence are some of the earliest naturalistic figure sculptures of the Renaissance.

NEW TECHNIQUES IN PAINTING

In painting, as opposed to sculpture, naturalism entailed more challenges for artists. The Florentine architect and scholar Leon Battista Alberti wrote a treatise (book) about painting in which he said it was the job of the painter to "represent things seen," so that people looking at a painting should feel almost as if they were looking at a scene through a window. He described a number of techniques that would help artists with the basic difficulty of depicting space and solid objects in a realistic way on a flat surface.

Perspective and realistic lighting were the two most important new techniques. Linear perspective is a mathematical system that enables artists to represent accurately the way that distant objects appear smaller than

those nearer us. The Florentine artist and architect Filippo Brunelleschi first developed linear perspective, and Alberti wrote about it in his treatise on painting. Masaccio was one of the first painters to apply the rules of linear perspective in wall paintings such as *The Holy Trinity* and those decorating the Brancacci Chapel.

Masaccio was also one of the first artists to realize that naturalistic light effects played an important part in making pictures look real. He used light and shadow to model objects, or make them look solid, and to unify the different elements shown in his pictures. Medieval painters had bathed their pictures in a uniform light, which made them look flat. They had also used light symbolically, most notably in the depiction of halos, the circles of

Above: **Saint Peter Healing the Sick** *(about 1427), one of Masaccio's frescoes in the Brancacci Chapel, Florence. Masaccio used perspective to create the effect of the street going back behind the figures and realistic light to model the people and create the shadows they cast on the ground.*

A DIFFERENT KIND OF NATURALISM

Naturalism played a key role in the work of artists in northern Europe, particularly those from Flanders (a region that includes present-day Belgium and parts of the Netherlands and France). However, there were important differences between the naturalistic art of the Italian and "Northern" Renaissance. Flemish artists concentrated on painting details of the physical world, and their pictures teem with everyday objects and intricate details. They often applied this approach to their portrayal of religious subjects, showing holy figures and Bible stories as if they were taking place in their own time, in homely settings and the countryside of northern Europe. Unlike Italian painters, who used elaborate rules and theories in the representation of the human form and real space, Flemish artists discovered naturalistic techniques by trial and error. They noticed, for example, how views look bluer and paler the further away they are, an effect known as "aerial perspective."

Right: **The Virgin Feeding the Christ Child with Porridge (about 1513) by the Flemish painter Gerard David.**

heavenly light used to denote holy figures. While Renaissance artists still painted halos, they also observed realistic light effects. For example, if the light source (maybe a window) was depicted on the left-hand side of the picture, the left side of everything shown was in bright light, while the right-hand side was in shadow, just as would be the case in the real world.

OIL PAINT AND OPTICAL DEVICES

Some artists also began to work in a new sort of paint that made it easier for them to create more lifelike pictures. This new material was oil paint, and it was first developed by Flemish painters in the early 15th century. Unlike other types of paint, it is slow-drying and so enables artists to spend time painting details and blending colors.

Some scholars now think that artists also used optical devices as early as the 15th century to help them achieve lifelike appearances in their pictures—

they certainly used them in the second half of the 16th century. These devices were variations on the *camera obscura*, an apparatus that consists of a dark room with a small hole in one side through which shines a beam of light from a brightly lit scene outside. The light forms an upside-down image that can be seen if a piece of paper is held up to it. Artists can then draw around this image before completing the drawing in the usual way. The projected image can be adjusted if the light is shone through a lens or reflected off a mirror. Alberti and Leonardo both wrote about the *camera obscura,* and artists as early as Jan van Eyck could have experimented with it.

The growth of naturalism can also be seen in the emergence of new types of picture in the Renaissance. Alongside religious subjects new sorts of painting based on accurate observation became popular, particularly realistic portraits and landscapes.

Navigation

The Renaissance is often called the age of exploration because it was the time when Europeans first discovered the Americas and other lands that lay beyond the known oceans. The mariners of the time performed extraordinary feats of navigation with the simplest instruments to help them. They set out on months-long voyages across the open seas armed with only magnetic compasses to determine direction and primitive devices to plot their course.

The long sea crossings were filled with danger. During medieval times ships had mainly kept close to shore, where seamen could navigate using coastal features. Now sailors ventured across waters where no ship had sailed before. To find their way, these hardy mariners used both traditional techniques and new instruments.

DEAD RECKONING

Medieval sailors venturing into open waters had used a process called dead reckoning to calculate their position. Dead reckoning was based on the distance sailed, the direction, and the effect of wind and sea currents. Experienced seafarers had a good knowledge of ocean currents, tides, and prevailing winds. Other clues such as clouds gathering on hills beyond the horizon and floating seaweed told sailors when they were nearing land.

From ancient times sailors had used the position of the sun and stars to work out their direction. By day the sun rose in the east, burned overhead at

midday, and set in the west. North and south could be worked out from the shadows cast at midday. Seamen also tracked the position of the sun across the sky to work out which way to go. At night mariners navigated by Polaris, the "Pole Star," which shone constantly in the north. In far northern waters Polaris appeared high in the sky. Closer to the equator it seemed much lower. Sailors could thus use the star's height to estimate their latitude—their distance north or south of the equator.

Since about 1200 A.D. European sailors had used magnetic compasses to follow a course or bearing. They had discovered that a magnetized iron needle allowed to move freely always pointed north–south. Early compasses consisted of a needle placed on a sliver

Above: A 16th-century astrolabe. The astrolabe was used by navigators to measure the altitude of the sun, from which they could determine their latitude, or distance from the equator.

of wood, floating in a bowl of water. By Renaissance times more sophisticated brass compasses had been developed, containing needles suspended on upright pivots. Such magnetic compasses were not entirely reliable. Sailors did not understand that the compass was reacting to the magnetic pull of the earth—they believed that the needle was attracted to the Pole Star. In reality a compass points not to the true north, but to the magnetic north, which is constantly shifting.

THE QUADRANT AND ASTROLABE

During the 15th and 16th centuries the introduction of several new aids made the process of navigation easier. An instrument called a quadrant helped sailors calculate their latitude by measuring the height of the Pole Star more accurately. Quadrants were shaped like a quarter-circle, with degrees marked around the curved edge, and had a weighted line attached to the right angle formed at the circle's center. Sight-holes along one edge allowed sailors to align the quadrant with the Pole Star. The angle that the weighted line made with the quadrant indicated the height of the star above the horizon and thus the ship's latitude. In rough weather, however, ships often pitched and heaved, causing the weighted line to swing wildly. That made quadrants difficult to use.

During the 15th century Portuguese instrument-makers developed another

Left: A 16th-century print showing one navigator (on the left) taking a sighting on the Pole Star with a cross-staff and another (on the right) using an astrolable to determine the height of the sun.

navigation aid, the seaman's astrolabe. It was used to take sightings from the sun or stars. The first astrolabes, which were invented by the ancient Greeks, were working models of the heavens. The seaman's astrolabe was simpler. It consisted of a disk with degrees marked around the edge and a rotating arm at the center—the arm was used to take sightings of the sun. The instrument was suspended from a rope or chain. At midday the navigator rotated the arm until it was aligned with the sun. The degree marked by the arm showed the sun's height and thus the ship's latitude —its distance from the equator.

In the 16th century a new instrument called the cross-staff was developed. As its name suggests, it was a staff with a movable crosspiece, which was used to measure the height of stars. Sailors lined up the staff with the horizon, then moved the crosspiece until its top edge was level with Polaris.

CALCULATING LONGITUDE

Quadrants, astrolabes, and cross-staffs all helped sailors calculate their latitude. Longitude, or the distance east or west from the meridian, is much harder to work out. Renaissance seamen estimated their east–west position by recording their progress on charts, but on long voyages this method became very inaccurate. Longitude can only be properly calculated with the help of an accurate clock to show the exact moment of midday, when the sun is at its highest. Clocks that could keep accurate time at sea were not invented until long after Renaissance times, in the 18th century.

Above: A magnetic compass made in 1568 by Nikolaus Rensperger. The compass is contained in an elaborate box made of gold, and the compass needle rotates on an upright pivot.

A RATE OF KNOTS

In order to measure the distance that they had traveled, sailors needed to be able to gauge how fast they were moving. In Renaissance times sailors calculated their ship's speed using a "log line"—literally a log attached to a long rope. The rope was marked with knots tied at regular intervals. Out at sea the log was tossed off the stern (back) of the boat and the rope cast out. Using a sand-filled hourglass, sailors counted how many knots were pulled out during a set period. In this way they were able to measure the ship's speed, or "rate of knots." Today we still measure the speed of ships and boats in knots rather than miles per hour. One knot is equivalent to 1.15mph (1.85 km/h).

SEE ALSO

♦ Exploration
♦ Maps and Mapmaking
♦ Ships

Neoplatonism

Above: A detail from The School of Athens, *painted by Raphael (1483–1520). The two central figures are the ancient Greek philosophers Plato (left) and his most famous student, Aristotle.*

In the 1460s the powerful Florentine banker Cosimo de Medici (1389–1464) gave a young Florentine scholar named Marsilio Ficino (1433–1499) two extraordinary gifts. The first, bestowed in 1462, was a manuscript of the complete works of Plato. The second, made the following year, was a country villa called Montevecchio. In return Ficino's task was to translate all of Plato's works from Greek into Latin.

Over the following years scholars, poets, and statesmen came to Montevecchio to study and discuss Plato and other classical (ancient Greek and Roman) writers. The villa became the center of the Platonic Academy of Florence—a kind of college of philosophy based on the Academy of ancient Athens where Plato had taught his ideas. The writings of Ficino and those of his followers like Giovanni Pico della Mirandola (1463–1494) were enormously influential, and by the 16th century this new Platonism had spread throughout Europe.

In the early 15th century a revival of interest in the works of the ancient Greek philosopher Plato (about 428–348 B.C.) led to an exciting new school of thought that we now call Neoplatonism ("New Platonism"). It encouraged people to believe in the immortal soul and each person's freedom to connect with an eternal world of universal values, such as truth, goodness, beauty, and love. These ideas quickly became fashionable and influenced art, literature, and humanist and Christian thinking.

PLATO'S WORLD OF IDEAS

Philosophers (thinkers) before Plato were primarily concerned with the world of material things around them that they could see, smell, and touch. Plato, however, came to believe in the existence of another reality—a world of ideas—beyond the material world. This reality was eternal and unchanging, and could be perceived only by the mind. It was from this eternal world that humankind derived its absolute values such as love, justice, and beauty. Plato also believed that all people had an immortal soul separate from their

Left: A detail from a painting by Domenico Ghirlandaio (1449–1494), which includes a portrait of Marsilio Ficino (on the left of the group). Ficino translated Plato's works from Greek into Latin, and his house was the center of the Platonic Academy of Florence, where Plato's works were eagerly studied and discussed.

material body. Plato set out his ideas in a series of imaginary *Dialogues* (conversations) between people holding different opinions.

PLOTINUS LEADS REVIVAL

Plato largely shaped later Greek and Roman thought, even though many individual thinkers disagreed with his ideas. In the third century A.D. the Roman philosopher Plotinus (205–270 A.D.) believed that Plato's philosophy had become corrupted and misunderstood. He led a revival of Platonic philosophy and developed many of its ideas into a new system of thought, called Neoplatonism. According to Plotinus, every human soul is part of an eternal and absolute reality, called the nous; but because of people's arrogance and love of material things the soul becomes corrupt. Nevertheless, humans can choose to reject the material world, allowing the soul to find its way back to the nous. People

experience this unity with the nous as a feeling of intense joy or liberation.

Plotinus's Neoplatonism greatly influenced early Christian thinkers. They, too, believed that human beings

PLATONIC LOVE

One of Ficino's most popular works was *De amore* ("On Love"). The work is a commentary on Plato's dialogue *Symposium*, but it is also a work of philosophy in its own right. In *De amore* Ficino drew a parallel between Platonic and Christian ideas about love. Following Plato, Ficino argued that love was a basic need of every human being and was the expression of a desire to be reunited with the ultimate reality or, in Christian terms, God. Sexual love was the lowest, or least worthy, form of this desire and risked trapping men and women in the corrupt material world. The highest form of love was a spiritual friendship based on a shared love of God.

Ficino's idea of spiritual love came to dominate the poetry and literature of 16th-century Europe. Even today we use the term "Platonic love" to describe a loving but nonsexual relationship between two people.

must renounce worldly "temptations" such as power and lust, and through prayer and fasting struggle to become reunited with God, whom they identified with the Neoplatonic nous.

CHRISTIAN CONNECTIONS

Many later Christian thinkers, however, were suspicious of the ideas of Plato and Plotinus because both philosophers were pagan (non-Christian). Renaissance Neoplatonic philosophers like Ficino continued to worry about this problem, and many of their writings deal with the struggle to reconcile Platonic and Christian ideas and so avoid the charge of heresy.

Below: A detail from the Adoration of the Magi *by Sandro Botticelli (1444–1510), showing Pico della Mirandola (with the red cap) in the center of the group. Pico was a follower of Ficino and helped spread Neoplatonic ideas in his writings.*

Soon after Ficino began work translating Plato's *Dialogues*, Cosimo de Medici brought him another Greek manuscript to translate. It was the *Poimandres* ("The Shepherd of Man"), which was thought to be by an ancient Greek thinker called Hermes Trismegistus. It had many similarities with the Old Testament. Ficino published his translation of the *Poimandres* in 1471, and it quickly became a bestseller. Armed with works such as this, Ficino and other humanists argued that there were links between biblical and classical thought. They believed that the ancient philosophers had written as truthfully if not as clearly as the biblical prophets and that their work contained Christian meanings. Ficino himself was able to lay aside his own doubts about his work and become a priest.

NEOPLATONIC HUMANISM

Ficino's translation of Plato's *Dialogues* was finally published in 1484, although scholars had been reading manuscript versions of the work much earlier. Ficino also published his own works on philosophy, the most important of which was the *Theologica Platonica* ("Platonic Theology," 1482). In it he argued—as Plotinus had before him—that the human soul was immortal. Traditional church teachings followed the ancient Greek philosopher Aristotle (384–322 B.C.) in saying that there was no such thing as the individual immortal soul. It was only in 1512—partly as a result of Ficino's work—that the concept became an accepted part of Christian belief.

The belief in the immortality of the human soul was part of a wider theme in Neoplatonic thought: the worth and dignity of every human being. This idea was at the heart of the writings of Ficino's follower, Pico della Mirandola, and at the heart of Renaissance humanism. In his *Oration on the Dignity of Man* Pico asserted that God had not fixed human nature as either good or evil, but had given each person the freedom to perfect themselves.

Other aspects of Neoplatonism were more mystical. Ficino himself was very interested in such matters as dreams, astrology, and magic. Such interests sometimes attracted the criticism of the church but nevertheless were an important reason why Neoplatonist ideas gained so much popularity. The notion of a secret, hidden order attracted many people living in what appeared to be a senseless, turbulent world threatened by war and plague.

ALL THE FASHION

Neoplatonic ideas became very fashionable at the Medici court and had a powerful influence on Renaissance art and literature in Florence. The most famous Neoplatonic painting is *Primavera* ("Spring") by Botticelli, which depicts classical gods and goddesses in a flower-strewn orchard. It is a symbolic illustration of Neoplatonic ideas, including the Neoplatonic concept of

> *Neoplatonic ideas had a powerful influence on Renaissance art and literature*

love. At the center of the painting is Venus, goddess of love, whom Ficino described as "born of Heaven and more than others beloved by God." Botticelli, like Ficino, attempted to reconcile classical and Christian views in his depiction of these classical figures.

By the 16th century Neoplatonic ideas had spread across Europe and become commonplace, especially in France and England. Many writers dealt with Neoplatonic themes. Love poetry, above all, often depicted a poet's struggle to transform human love into a spiritual communion of souls. The French poet Pierre de Ronsard (1524–1585), for example, declared in one sonnet: "To fly away to the heavens, I want to burn away all the imperfection of my human skin."

Neoplatonism continued to inspire European thought, art, and literature for centuries, right up to the present day. However, from the 18th century onward many thinkers and writers attacked both it and Platonism in general for their obscurity, mysticism, and lack of rationality.

Above: A detail from Botticelli's **Primavera,** *showing the goddess Venus (center) with Flora on the right. Venus represents earthly and spiritual love, while Flora represents beauty.*

SEE ALSO

♦ Botticelli
♦ Classicism
♦ Courts and Court Culture
♦ Florence
♦ Humanism
♦ Medici Family

Netherlands

Above: Prince William the Silent of Orange, who led a successful rebellion against Spanish rule of the Low Countries.

At the start of the Renaissance the area that we know today as the Netherlands was not a united region. It was made up of a number of independent counties and duchies, such as Holland, Utrecht, and Gelderland. The name Netherlands means "Low Countries," and in the Renaissance this term was used not only to describe the counties of the present-day Netherlands but also the prosperous regions that lay to the south, such as Artois and Flanders.

At the end of the 14th century the provinces of the Low Countries were busy, well-populated, and generally prosperous. The territory was crossed by a network of waterways, including the great Rhine and Meuse rivers, which provided a transport system to support the massive amount of international commerce that took place in the region. The most important trade was that in woolen cloth, a valuable commodity that was exported all over the known world. Imports included wine, silk, spices, and grain.

Flemish cities like Ghent, Antwerp, and Bruges were great international marketplaces and supported large communities of foreigners. The cities were extremely prosperous and attracted artists and craftsmen who created outstanding paintings, carvings, jewelry, and fine wares that wealthy merchants could afford to buy.

The northern provinces were not quite so dominated by big cities and trade, though there too towns were growing rapidly. The Dutch—the Germanic-speaking people who lived in the north—also had a successful cloth trade, but in addition they had other major industries, particularly preserving herring, brewing beer, refining salt, and building ships.

RISE OF BURGUNDY

In the 15th century the political situation in the Low Countries changed as the area came under foreign control. In 1369 Margaret of Flanders, the heiress to the county, had married Duke Philip the Bold of Burgundy.

When Margaret's father died in 1384, Philip became the ruler of four very important provinces—Artois, Rethel, Flanders, and Nevers. Once they had secured a power base in this area, the Burgundians began to expand their influence. Over the next century they managed to gain control over Brabant, Hainaut, Holland, and Gelderland as well. They did so by a combination of marriage, conquest, inheritance, and political negotiation.

Successive 15th-century dukes tried to introduce new restrictions on the freedom of government enjoyed by the cities and provinces. They appointed their own Burgundian governors and other state officials, and established a strong central government that could impose decisions on the local governing bodies and overrule their traditional privileges. This policy caused a great deal of resentment.

THE STATES GENERAL

In 1477 an assembly known as the States General managed to negotiate an agreement with Duchess Mary of Burgundy. The assembly consisted of representatives from all the various provinces that made up the Burgundian union. The agreement confirmed the provinces' rights to impose tolls and levy taxes, to control currency, to wage war, and to conduct government business and administer the law in Dutch and not French. The agreement was the first written constitution for the Low Countries and remained a respected and influential document for centuries.

The situation changed dramatically in the 16th century, a time of great upheaval across northern Europe. In the same year that she signed the agreement with the States General, Mary of Burgundy had married Max-imilian of Hapsburg, the future Holy Roman emperor. Through their son Philip I (1478–1506) the Burgundian lands became part of a huge empire that also included Austria and Spain. The empire was engaged in a constant power struggle with France, and the Low Countries became involved in several of its wars. The Hapsburgs were also in favor of strong central government and took steps to reduce the power of the States General.

SPREAD OF PROTESTANTISM

During the reign of Philip's son Charles V (ruled 1519–1556) the struggles against the Hapsburgs took on a religious dimension. In the decades following the publication of Martin Luther's 95 theses in 1517, Protestantism spread quickly across the Low Countries. By far the most popular and influential group of Protestants were the Calvinists, who were followers of the radical French religious thinker John Calvin (1509–1564). His idea that people can show their worship of God simply by working hard appealed to Dutch society.

Below: This map shows the area covered by the seven counties that made up the United Provinces of the Netherlands, as well as some of the most important regions to the south.

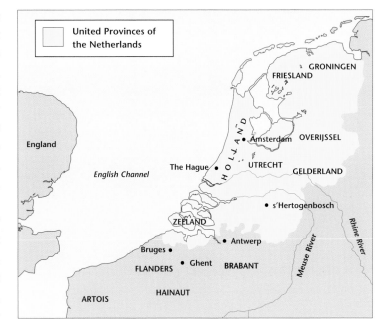

Charles attempted to stamp out Protestantism by force, and many Calvinists were persecuted for heresy, or holding views that were contrary to church doctrine. Some were tortured and killed. The persecution continued under Charles' son Philip II of Spain (ruled 1556–1598), and resentment toward the Catholic church became entwined with anger at Spanish rule. In 1566 this resentment reached a climax with a series of riots and attacks on Catholic churches across the country.

Philip retaliated by sending in an army of Spanish soldiers led by his general Fernando Alvarez de Toledo, the third duke of Alba. Alba's objective was to stamp out the Protestants using brutal force. He quickly became known for his cruelty. In the major towns

AMSTERDAM

Above: Amsterdam in the 17th century. After its rapid growth in importance in the late 16th century Amsterdam went on to dominate north European trade.

The city of Amsterdam grew rapidly during the Renaissance, eventually overtaking Antwerp as the richest and most influential city in the Low Countries. As late as the 13th century Amsterdam was little more than a small fishing village, but it grew steadily over the course of the next 200 years, prospering through shipping and trade.

The real explosion in the city's fortunes came toward the end of the 16th century, when Antwerp fell into Spanish hands, and many of the town's Protestant bankers and merchants fled north to Amsterdam. Shortly afterward there was another influx of wealthy new inhabitants—this time Jewish traders trying to escape from oppression in Portugal and Eastern Europe. In the 17th century Amsterdam became the most important trading city in Europe. It was also the continent's chief financial center, thanks in part to the establishment of the Exchange Bank of Amsterdam, which allowed merchants to trade currency at established rates.

Left: This engraving shows Spanish troops being put to flight by a force of Sea Beggars during the Low Countries' revolt against Spain in the 16th century. The Sea Beggars were Dutch pirates who waged a hit-and-run war against the Spanish.

councils were set up to try people for heresy. Alba also introduced a new system of taxation that increased Spanish control over the region.

WILLIAM OF ORANGE

The result of Alba's measures was open rebellion. The revolt was led by Prince William the Silent of Orange (1533–1584). The rebels used hit-and-run tactics and at first had limited success. However, in 1572 they succeeded in capturing the strategically crucial port of Brielle, and after that they gained control of most of the Dutch north. In 1579 all the northern provinces and some of the southern ones joined together in an alliance against Spain known as the Union of Utrecht.

Prince William worked hard to unify all the provinces of the Low Countries, but he could not make them remain in agreement. The southern cities and provinces were less opposed to Spain and Catholicism than their northern counterparts and soon broke away. The seven northern provinces—Holland, Zeeland, Utrecht, Gelderland, Overijssel, Freisland, and Groningen—declared themselves an independent nation, known as the United Provinces of the Netherlands.

War with Spain intensified, and the new nation suffered many losses, including Prince William of Orange, who was assassinated in 1584. The provinces soon found an important ally, however. England was now also at war with Spain and sent troops to help fight in the Netherlands. In 1588 the Spanish suffered a huge setback when the great Armada (or fleet) that they sent to invade England was defeated in battle and then destroyed by storms.

By 1600 all Spanish troops had been forced out of the provinces of the Netherlands, though the war dragged on until 1648, when the Spanish finally recognized the sovereignty of the United Provinces. This small republic had triumphed against the most powerful European nation. It went on to its own golden age of greatness and power in the 17th and 18th centuries.

Orthodox Church

Around 1400 the main religious division in the Christian world was between Roman Catholicism in the West and the Orthodox church in Eastern Europe and the Middle East. As the Islamic Ottoman armies advanced on the historic Orthodox city of Constantinople, the two churches attempted to reunite to repel the threat of Muslim invasion. However, it was too late to save Constantinople. Its fall was to have important consequences for the future of the Orthodox church and for Renaissance Europe.

The Orthodox church is sometimes called the Eastern Orthodox church or Greek Orthodox church. That is because it is directly descended from the churches established during the early Christian period in the eastern, Greek-speaking half of the Roman Empire. The empire in the Latin-speaking West collapsed, but the East Roman Empire survived for a thousand years, down to the 15th century. During this later phase historians call it Byzantium, or the Byzantine Empire. Its capital, Constantinople, was for many centuries the greatest city in the world; and its bishop, the patriarch of Constantinople, became the head of the Orthodox church.

DOCTRINAL DISPUTES

For centuries the Christian churches in the West and East remained united despite their different languages and ways of life. But by the ninth century the differences between the two

churches meant that they had drifted far apart. As well as customs and ceremonies the two churches disagreed over issues that both sides thought of as vital, including points of doctrine and whether priests could marry.

The disputes were sharpened by the pope's claim to rule the entire church; that was unacceptable in the East, where regional churches were self-governing and even the patriarch of Constantinople was an honorary leader rather than a ruler. In 1054 the situation deteriorated, and the two churches officially broke off relations. The Orthodox church and the Roman Catholic church were now separate and hostile institutions. Then, in 1204, western crusaders sacked Constan-

Above: A 15th-century print of Constantinople. The city was the center of the Orthodox church until it was conquered by the Ottoman Turks in May 1453.

tinople and for a time set up "Latin" kingdoms in place of the Byzantine Empire. Eventually, the Latins were driven out, leaving a legacy of hatred and distrust of Catholicism.

MUSLIM INVASIONS

Over the centuries the geography of the Orthodox world changed greatly. The Byzantine Empire gradually shrank under Muslim assaults, but in the ninth and 10th centuries the Slav peoples of the Balkans (southeastern Europe), eastern Europe, and Russia—a vast area—converted from paganism to Orthodox Christianity.

As the Byzantine Empire grew weaker, its emperors realized it could only survive with help from the West. That meant trying to bring about a reconciliation between the Roman Catholic church and the Orthodox church. An attempt was made as early

---

The Slav peoples of the Balkans, Eastern Europe, and Russia converted from paganism to Christianity

---

as 1274 at the Council of Lyons, but the agreement that was reached was rejected by both the clergy and the people of Constantinople.

By 1400 the situation had become desperate. The Muslim Ottoman Turks had conquered Anatolia (present-day Turkey) and much of the Balkans, reducing the Byzantine Empire to a small area around the city of Constantinople. The Byzantines again tried to end the schism (religious split) in the hope of receiving military aid, and in 1438–1439 a joint church council

ICONS

Icons are Christian images that were, and are, especially important in the Orthodox church. They are usually paintings on wooden panels depicting Jesus, the Virgin Mary, or some other holy person such as a saint. In Orthodox churches the altar is separated from the congregation by the iconostasis, a screen that is covered with icons. But icons are also found in Orthodox homes, and the objects themselves are regarded as sanctified; famous icons are said to have performed many miracles. The painting style has always been in the Byzantine tradition—not "realistic" but aiming to communicate a solemn and timeless feeling.

Above: A 15th-century Russian icon showing Christ enthroned. Icons were thought to be sacred objects that in some cases were capable of performing miracles.

was held at Ferrara and Florence in Italy. The Byzantines were in a weak bargaining position and gave way on most points, and in July 1439 the council proclaimed the reunion of West and East.

The union failed because of the strength of popular feeling against it

However, the union failed because of the strength of popular feeling against it. As the Ottoman assault reached its climax, the Emperor Constantine XI Palaeologus vainly made the official proclamation of the union in Constantinople in December 1452. But no help arrived, and on May 29, 1453, the Turks stormed the city. The emperor, together with the Byzantine Empire, perished.

All the Greek-speaking lands and the Balkans were now under Muslim rule. But although there were many conversions to Islam, the Orthodox church survived. Meanwhile, the fall of Constantinople had a particularly strong impact on Russia, where the grand dukes of Moscow (then called Muscovy) were gradually uniting the

SEE ALSO

♦ Catholic Church
♦ Constantinople
♦ Eastern Europe
♦ Islam
♦ Ottoman Empire
♦ Religious Themes in Art
♦ Russia

Below: Saint Basil's Cathedral in Moscow, built in the 16th century after Russia became the center of the Orthodox church.

country. Now the most powerful of the remaining Orthodox states, Moscow began to be seen as the successor to Byzantium, an impression reinforced in 1472, when the Russian ruler Ivan III married the niece of the last Byzantine emperor. A belief developed that Moscow was "the Third Rome" (after Rome and Constantinople) and as such the center of Orthodoxy, with a mission to protect the faith everywhere. This missionary sense, and the Byzantine-style power of Russia's rulers, influenced the country's development right up to modern times.

The Renaissance in the West was strongly influenced by Orthodox scholarship in the early 15th century. The Council of Florence led to important contacts, including a visit to the city by Gemistus Pletho, a learned Byzantine whose lectures introduced Florence to the works of the ancient Greek philosopher Plato and inspired the Neoplatonism of Marsilio Ficino. Later, scholars fleeing from the East brought with them manuscripts of other ancient Greek writers.

Ottoman Empire

Below: This 16th-century miniature shows the Ottoman sultan Süleyman the Magnificent hunting. It was under Süleyman's reign that the Ottomans reached the height of their power.

At the time of the European Renaissance the Ottoman Empire was one of the most powerful states in the world. By the mid-16th century it stretched across three continents, from present-day Iraq in the east to Algeria in the west. Its rulers, who bore the title of sultan, were great military leaders as well as important patrons of Muslim art.

The founder of the Ottoman dynasty, or family of rulers, was a Muslim Turkic prince named Osman I (1258–about 1326), who originally ruled over

a small territory in Anatolia, or present-day Turkey. For many centuries Anatolia had belonged to Byzantium—the great Christian empire whose capital was at Constantinople. In the 12th century, however, Muslim Turkic peoples from Central Asia conquered much of the region.

At the head of the invasion were Muslim warriors called ghazis. One of their religious duties was to conquer non-Muslim lands. The ghazis took advantage of the weakness of Byzantium to seize more and more of its territory, and by 1300 the Byzantine Empire had lost almost all its lands in Asia. Much of the newly conquered lands lay in the hands of Osman, who had quickly come to dominate other ghazi rulers.

BALKAN INVASION

The Ottoman conquests continued under the rule of Osman's son Orhan (ruled 1326–1362). In 1356 Orhan launched a successful invasion of the Byzantine province of Thrace. Orhan encouraged Turkic peoples to settle the new lands. Christian inhabitants who offered no resistance to the Ottomans were usually allowed to keep their religion and rights. Those who resisted were killed, enslaved, or forced to convert. Constantinople was now almost totally encircled by Ottoman lands. Without siege equipment, however, Orhan realized he had little chance of breaching the Byzantine capital's walls.

Orhan built up a powerful new army made up of two main parts. The

Right: This map shows the size of the Ottoman Empire at three key points in its history: the fall of Constantinople in 1453; the end of the reign of Süleyman the Magnificent in 1566; and the siege of Vienna in 1683.

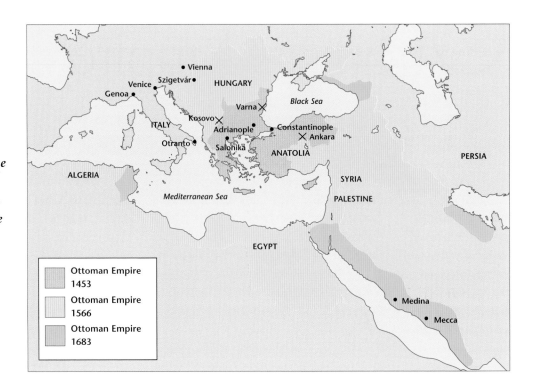

first part was a militia of Turkic men who were given land in return for military service. The second part was an elite band of paid infantry (foot soldiers), known as the janissary corps, composed largely of Christian or recently converted slaves. There was often tension between the two groups, as Muslim Turks and Christians vied for power in the growing empire.

WAR ON TWO FRONTS

Orhan's son Murad I (ruled 1360–1389) was another brilliant and ambitious military leader. In 1362 he conquered Byzantium's second most important city, Adrianople (present-day Edirne), and made it the new Ottoman capital. From Adrianople Murad launched invasions of the nearby Christian kingdoms of Serbia and Bulgaria, and in 1389 the Turkish and Serbian armies met on the plain of Kosovo. Before the battle a Christian soldier came to Murad's tent, pretending to be a deserter, and stabbed the Ottoman ruler in the heart.

It was left to Murad's son Bayezid I (ruled 1389–1402) to lead the Ottoman troops to victory.

Bayezid was even more ambitious than his father. For a decade he fought successful wars on both the European and Anatolian borders of his kingdom. He roundly defeated the Hungarians, who led a crusade, or holy war, against him and one by one he defeated the last remaining Turkish principalities in Anatolia. He was held in such high esteem in the Muslim world that the caliph of Cairo, one of the highest authorities in the Muslim world, awarded him the title of sultan.

Bayezid was prevented from seizing Constantinople only by an invasion from the east. The Mongol ruler Tamerlane (1336–1405) had founded a mighty empire in Asia, stretching from the Mediterranean to the borders of India and China. He saw the Ottoman empire as a threat to his own and was determined to crush it. In 1402 he led a massive army into Anatolia, and on July 25 he defeated the Ottomans at

Ankara and took Bayezid prisoner. According to legend, the Ottoman ruler was held captive in a golden cage until he killed himself in 1403.

WAR WITH VENICE

Bayezid's death was the starting point of a decline in the fortunes of the Ottoman Empire. For more than a decade Bayezid's sons fought each other for power. In 1413 one of them, Mehmed I (ruled 1413–1421), finally managed to restore order to the empire. His eldest son and successor, Murad II (ruled 1421–1444 and 1446–1451), was forced to wage almost continuous war during his long reign. In particular he came into conflict with Venice, which controlled many islands in the eastern Mediterranean. By 1430

Murad had built a fleet big enough to take the Venetian port of Salonika and force Venice to sign a peace treaty.

In 1444 Murad abdicated his throne to his young son Mehmed II (ruled 1444–1446 and 1451–1481). The pope in Rome seized the opportunity to launch a new crusade against the Ottomans. European troops marched through Serbia to the Black Sea but then began to quarrel. That gave Murad time gather an army and defeat the Europeans at Varna on November 10, 1444. The crusade was the last full-scale European attempt to curb the growth of the Ottoman Empire for several centuries.

Murad retook the throne and during the last years of his reign established his rule across much of

Left: This painting by the Venetian artist Palma Giovane shows Ottoman troops attacking the walls of Constantinople in 1453. The city finally fell after a siege of almost two months.

CHRISTIAN SOLDIERS

During his reign Murad II reformed the janissary wing of his army. He introduced a system (known as *devsirme*) whereby Christian families living in his empire could be forced to hand over one of their sons to Ottoman officials. The boys were bought up as Muslims in special schools where they sometimes trained as civil servants but more often as janissary soldiers. The reformed janissaries were famed for their courage and skill and for their absolute devotion to the sultan. They were forbidden to marry and lived in their own quarters. The janissaries were the first to breach the city walls during the siege of Constantinople.

Below: The interior of the Topkapi palace in Istanbul, which was home to the Ottoman sultans. The palace was famous for its splendor.

southeast Europe. His subjects—both Muslim and Christian—respected him for his administrative skills and sense of justice, which contrasted with the corruption and incompetence of the Byzantine rulers.

When Murad died in 1451, his son Mehmed took the throne for a second time. He was determined to conquer Constantinople and destroy Byzantium once and for all. On April 6, 1453 he laid siege to the city, using heavy artillery to bombard its defenses. Despite a valiant defence led by Emperor Constantine XI, the Ottomans finally breached the city walls. Troops poured into the city and began an orgy of pillage and murder. On the afternoon of May 29 Mehmed rode into the city and restored peace.

OTTOMAN ISTANBUL

Mehmed made Constantinople his new capital. It came to be known as "the City," or Istanbul. Under the last Byzantine emperors the city had fallen into disrepair, and the sultan now rebuilt the city's walls, streets, bridges, and buildings, returning it to much of its old splendor. He encouraged communities from every religion to establish themselves in Istanbul and allowed them to follow their own laws and traditions. Meanwhile, Mehmed also strengthened his empire. Like his father, the sultan relied on a team of ministers, called viziers, to supervise its day-to-day affairs. The team was headed by a chief minister called the grand vizier.

After the fall of Constantinople Europeans began to fear an Ottoman invasion. In 1480 their fears seemed about to be realized when the Ottoman fleet destroyed the port of Otranto in southern Italy. Only the death of Mehmed stopped the Ottomans from taking this invasion of Italy farther.

However, the relationship between the Ottoman Empire and Europe was not always hostile. For example, although the Ottomans spent much of the 15th century at war with Venice, the periods of peace saw a tremendous amount of trade between the two powers. Ottoman merchants also dealt extensively with the city of Genoa and many other European states. Because

the empire lay between Europe and East Asia, Ottoman traders were able to act as middlemen, becoming rich from the flow of spices westward and textiles eastward. Many European traders who traveled to Istanbul during the Renaissance gave admiring accounts of the Turks' religious tolerance and the sophistication of their culture.

Under Mehmed II's successors, Bayezid II (ruled 1481–1512) and Selim I (ruled 1512–1520), the Ottoman Empire continued to grow. In 1517 it doubled in size when Selim overthrew another Muslim empire, that of the Mamluks. The Mamluk dynasty had ruled Egypt, Palestine, and Syria for more than 250 years. The defeat of the Mamluks provided the Ottoman sultans with new sources of revenue and made the Ottoman Empire one of the wealthiest and most powerful states of the 16th century.

HEIGHT OF OTTOMAN POWER

The reign of Selim's son Süleyman I (ruled 1520–1566) was the most glorious period of Ottoman history. His reputation led Europeans to call him the "Magnificent," although the Ottoman Turks themselves referred to him as the "Lawgiver" because he introduced so many important reforms to their society.

During his reign Süleyman came into conflict with the rising empire of the Christian Hapsburg dynasty of central Europe. In 1529 Süleyman laid siege to the Hapsburg capital, Vienna, and seized control of Hungary. Süleyman also waged war in the east against Persia and its rulers, the Safavids. In 1555 the two Muslim powers agreed on a peace under which the Ottomans allowed Persian pilgrims to visit the holy cities. Wars in Europe continued to occupy Süleyman until

Left: This manuscript illustration shows Ottoman astronomers working in the royal observatory. It was built for the sultan Murad III in the 16th century.

the end of his reign, and he died while laying siege to the Hungarian city of Szigetvár in 1566.

After the death of Süleyman Ottoman power gradually declined. The increased use of alternative trade routes to East Asia by European merchants loosened the Ottomans' grip on international trade. Most of the sultans who came after Süleyman lacked the ability of their predecessors, and power struggles among the *devsirme* class weakened the empire considerably in the 17th century.

The decline of the Ottoman Empire was an extremely slow process, however. The empire continued to be a considerable force in the Eastern Mediterranean for over 350 years after its height in the reign of Süleyman, and in 1683 the Ottomans were powerful enough to once again besiege the city of Vienna. The final Ottoman emperor reigned until 1922, when the empire was dissolved and the present-day state of Turkey formed.

SEE ALSO

♦ Constantinople
♦ Hapsburg Family
♦ Holy Roman Empire
♦ Islam
♦ Orthodox Church
♦ Venice
♦ Warfare

Padua

PATAVIA

The town of Padua in northern Italy prospered during the Middle Ages, subduing neighboring cities and growing in political and economic importance. Padua was governed by the Carrara family from 1318 to 1405 and was then absorbed into the Venetian Empire. In the 15th and 16th centuries, under Venetian rule, Padua continued to flourish as an artistic center and a birthplace of the "new learning"—humanism.

While Genoa and Pisa represented the economic power of early Renaissance Italy, the first flowering of humanism started in Bologna and Padua. The two cities were the sites of Italy's first and second oldest universities respectively. The early humanists, who studied there, called their philosophy the "new learning." It was actually the re-discovery of old learning, since it involved the study of classical poetry and history as well as legal writings freshly translated from forgotten manuscripts. By the 15th century

Padua University had a large student body and had expanded to include schools of medicine, the arts, and science, as well as law.

RULERS OF PADUA

Padua had one of the first popular governments (communes) in Italy, as well as being an important artistic center between the 12th and 14th centuries. During the early 14th century it was torn apart by internal conflicts between supporters of the pope and those of the Holy Roman emperor before coming under the control of the Carrara family. Originally powerful landlords, the Carrara became one of Italy's first families to have their power recognized and authorized by the emperor, ruling Padua between 1318 and 1405.

In 1405 Padua was invaded and absorbed into the Venetian Empire. Venice, its dominant neighbor and one of Italy's most powerful city-states, was engaged in a campaign of mainland expansion, seeking to secure its trading

Above: A print of Padua from the Liber Chronicarum *("Chronicle of the World"), which was compiled by the German humanist Hartmann Schedel in July 1493. Schedel studied medicine at Padua University from 1463 to 1466.*

THE UNIVERSITY OF PADUA

The University of Padua was established in 1222 by a body of teachers and students who left the overcrowded Bologna University to found their own center of learning. By 1300 its reputation was drawing students from across Italy and Europe. Dante was a student there and, later, Petrarch. Originally a school of law, the university expanded under Venetian rule to include faculties of medicine, science, and the arts.

During the 15th and 16th centuries Padua was regarded as one of the leading universities of Renaissance Europe, especially in classical studies and scientific experimentation. The university counted many famous Renaissance humanists and scientists among its professors, including Andreas Vesalius (1514–1564), professor of surgery, and Galileo Galilei (1564–1642), professor of mathematics.

In 1545 the Venetian senate established Europe's first botanical garden at the university to help the study of herbal medicine. Around the same time, Vesalius made Padua the center for anatomy with his popular public demonstrations of dissections of dead

Above: The anatomy theater built at Padua University in about 1594 to hold the many students wanting to watch the dissections carried out there.

bodies. His groundbreaking work *On the Structure of the Human Body* (1543) used a combination of scientific method and detailed illustrations to describe the workings of the human body.

routes over the Alps into western Europe and ensure steady food supplies from the nearby farmlands.

Despite being a subject city, Padua continued to flourish and was largely left to govern itself. In 1509 Padua took advantage of Venice's temporary weakness to revolt against its overlords, as did many of Venice's other mainland possessions. The revolt was swiftly put down, and Padua remained under Venetian control until 1797.

ARTISTS IN PADUA

Padua's leading artist was Andrea Mantegna (1431–1506), a native Paduan, who painted the (now largely destroyed) frescoes at the Eremitani church in Padua before moving to the Gonzaga court at Mantua. Mantegna was much influenced by the international society of Padua—the

university attracted scholars from all over Italy and Europe. He was also inspired by Donatello's huge equestrian statue of Gattamelata (a mercenary Venetian general from Padua), which was put up outside the basilica in Padua in 1453.

The Florentine sculptor Donatello (1386–1466) was one of a number of artists who were attracted to Padua. Another was Giotto (about 1266–1337), who provided frescoes, statues, and reliefs for the six-domed Basilica di Sant'Antonio. The impressive basilica was built to house the bones of Saint Anthony of Padua, a wandering Franciscan friar. Giotto also produced work for the Scrovegni Chapel, which was built by a moneylender in the hope of escaping the eternal damnation in hell that was promised him in Dante's poem *The Divine Comedy*.

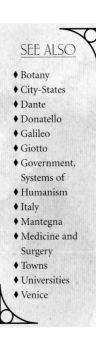

Painting

Renaissance paintings are some of the world's most famous works of art. During the 15th and 16th centuries painting was transformed by new techniques and new attitudes to human life. These developments were centered in Italy and culminated in the masterpieces of Leonardo da Vinci, Michelangelo, Raphael, and Titian.

Like other arts, painting reflected the Italian Renaissance belief in the value of the human personality and human achievement, and in the beauty and interest of the natural world. Though the change was gradual, this belief was one of the factors that made the Renaissance different from the Middle Ages. Religious art remained important, but scenes by Renaissance artists showing the Virgin and Child, the story of Jesus, or the lives of saints laid more emphasis on the human emotions and conflicts involved.

As artists expressed the human dimension of these scenes, they began to use greater naturalism: that is, a more accurate, lifelike rendering of people, events, and settings. This humanizing tendency was encouraged by the Renaissance admiration for the human-centered culture of ancient Greece and Rome (antiquity). Almost no Greek or Roman paintings survived in the Renaissance, although ancient descriptions stressed their lifelike qualities. Many antique sculptures did

Above: Raphael's **The Disputation of the Divine Sacrament** *(1508–1511), one of a series of frescoes painted to decorate three rooms in the papal apartments of the Vatican, Rome. Raphael's frescoes, known as the* **Stanze** *(Italian for "rooms"), are some of the greatest paintings made in the Renaissance.*

survive, and even more were dug up during building work in the 15th and 16th centuries. They were masterpieces of naturalism that glorified the nude (unclothed) human form. Renaissance painters like Michelangelo and Titian followed their example, making the nude—mostly neglected during the Middle Ages—one of the principal subjects of art. What was known of antique art also encouraged Renaissance painters to concentrate on portraying "noble" or physically splendid human forms rather than the less-than-perfect bodies of "ordinary" people. That is why their art, though naturalistic, is described as "idealized."

A NEW STYLE

Renaissance painting is often traced back to the Florentine artist Giotto (about 1266–1337), who was at the height of his powers early in the 14th century. He was one of the first artists to move away from the flat, stylized (artificial-looking) style of painting that characterized medieval art across Europe. Giotto's frescoes (wall paintings made on wet, or "fresh," plaster) were revolutionary in the way they presented well-characterized people and moments of intense drama.

As a general movement in the visual arts, the Renaissance did not begin until the early 15th century in Florence. In painting the key figure was Masaccio (1401–1428). Although he died when he was only 27 years old, his frescoes showed a renewed interest in depicting scenes in a lifelike way. Frescoes like *The Tribute Money* (about 1427) show his fresh approach, in which solidly modeled figures interact and convey a sense of the unfolding story through their gestures.

To paint people and scenes in a lifelike manner, artists learned to use new techniques. Masaccio employed linear perspective, which had just been worked out by his fellow Florentine, the architect Filippo Brunelleschi. It is a mathematical system that provides painters with a precise method of picturing on a flat surface how the eye sees a three-dimensional scene. Artists also studied the anatomy and proportions of the human body, and the effects of light on a scene.

All through the 15th century most of the leading painters came from Florence, among them Fra Angelico, Paolo Uccello, Sandro Botticelli, and Piero della Francesca, who worked outside the city. They all had their own

Below: Masaccio's fresco **The Tribute Money** *(about 1427) in the Brancacci Chapel, Florence. Masaccio shows three episodes from a bible story in which Christ (center) tells Saint Peter that he will find money to pay the tax man in the mouth of the first fish he catches. On the left Saint Peter is shown kneeling at the water's edge to take the coin from the fish's mouth, and on the right he gives it to the tax man.*

Left: **The Ghent Altarpiece** *(1432) by Jan van Eyck. God is shown in the center at the top, with Mary on the left and Saint John the Baptist on the right. To either side are pictures of angels and Adam and Eve. The scenes below show the bible story of the adoration of the lamb. The minute detail with which they are painted typifies northern European art.*

individual styles, and painting did not develop in a single direction. There were many innovations in Florentine painting, including the development of realistic portraiture and the acceptance of ancient Greek and Roman myths as subject matter for large-scale works.

In the later 15th century the Renaissance spread into northern Italy, where the outstanding painter was Andrea Mantegna. He was particularly influenced by ancient Roman history, and his historical scenes were so painstakingly researched that they have been described as "archaeological."

PAINTING IN NORTHERN EUROPE

Although the Renaissance is most closely associated with Italian art, important developments also took place in northern European painting. Like Italy, Flanders (a region that includes present-day Belgium and parts of the Netherlands and France) was evolving a prosperous town-based society in which painting flourished.

The greatest Flemish painter was Jan van Eyck. During the 1430s he produced masterpieces like *The Ghent Altarpiece* (1432) and *The Arnolfini Marriage* (1434), works remarkable for their minute detail and glowing colors. Van Eyck's meticulous observation of surface appearances characterizes Flemish art, but it differs from the naturalism of Italian artists, who were also concerned to understand the underlying structure of the natural world and to idealize appearances. Van Eyck was the first artist to develop the use of oil paint, and his fame helped spread the technique to Italy. There it was pioneered by Antonello da Messina and, toward the end of the 15th century, was taken up by Leonardo da Vinci and painters in Venice.

THE HIGH RENAISSANCE

The subtleties of oil paint were exploited to the full by Leonardo in paintings such as the *Mona Lisa* (1503–1506), which is probably the most famous picture in the world. Leonardo is one of the great figures of the period known as the "High Renaissance," which lasted for about 30 years after 1500. As its name suggests, the High Renaissance was in many respects the culmination of everything that had gone before. The techniques involved in naturalistic painting had been completely mastered. Set against convincing backgrounds, ambitious projects were carried out with apparent ease. Noble images of men and women were arranged in balanced compositions that gave a sense of harmony even to scenes of violent action or emotion. The most complex works breathed a spirit of grand simplicity that seemed typical of the age.

GREAT RENAISSANCE MASTERS

Leonardo was one of three artists whose achievements dominated the High Renaissance; the other two were Michelangelo (1475–1564) and Raphael (1483–1520). Though painting was only one of his skills, Michelangelo created the most colossal Renaissance work by a single individual: the frescoes on the ceiling of the Sistine Chapel in Rome (1508–1512). Michelangelo's turbulent spirit was apparent even during the High Renaissance; by contrast, Raphael's work seemed to embody a serene, harmonious spirit.

The great center of the arts during the High Renaissance was Rome, where the popes' lavish building and decorative projects offered unequaled opportunities for artists to exercise their skills. However, in 1527 the sack of Rome by German mercenaries dealt the papacy a terrible blow, and that year is sometimes said to mark the end of the High Renaissance. Wider changes in the political and religious climate of Italy may also have influenced artists, giving rise to more emotional and anxious attitudes. Alternatively, the very perfection of the High Renaissance may have persuaded a younger generation to move on and adopt other means of expression.

Whatever the reason, Italian painting after about 1530 abandoned High Renaissance ideals and used Renaissance techniques in a very different spirit. This new approach took a variety of forms, often involving deliberately fanciful elements or consciously unusual set-piece scenes with agitated or showy poses. Art historians have used the label "mannerism" to describe works of this type painted by such artists as Parmigianino, Agnolo Bronzino, and Jacopo da Pontormo.

In one Italian city-state the history of painting took a different course. The Renaissance came late to Venice—at

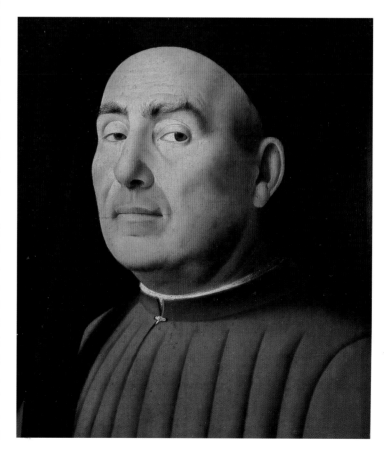

Below: This picture is thought to be a self-portrait by Antonello da Messina (about 1430–1479), who pioneered the use of oil paint in Italy. Although scholars used to think that Antonello studied in Flanders under Jan van Eyck, they now believe he trained in Naples, where Flemish influence on art was strong.

Left: Titian's **The Entombment of Christ** *(1559) was painted for King Philip II of Spain. The picture's loose brushwork and warm colors typify Venetian art.*

the end of the 15th century—and survived longer there than elsewhere in Italy. In the hands of Giovanni Bellini, Giorgione, Titian, and Paolo Veronese a distinctive Venetian style of painting developed. While the Florentines were master draftsmen, clearly outlining the figures and objects in their pictures, the Venetians adopted a more "painterly" style. The damp climate of their city made fresco, the most highly regarded painting technique elsewhere in Italy, an unsuitable material because plaster deteriorates in wet conditions. Instead, artists in Venice developed oil painting techniques, using brilliant colors and increasingly free brush work that became hallmarks of Venetian art.

THE SPREAD OF ITALIAN IDEAS

Italian Renaissance painting only made its impact on the rest of Europe in the 16th century. The German painter Albrecht Dürer was conscious that the Italians had "secret" knowledge and sought it on his visits to the country in 1497 and 1505–1507. Hans Holbein brought the Renaissance art of portraiture to England; other German painters, including Dürer himself and Grünewald, combined Renaissance techniques with distinctive northern traits. King Francis I of France pressed Leonardo da Vinci into living in France and later imported Italian artists to decorate his palace at Fontainebleau. Renaissance forms also gradually came to dominate Flemish painting. From the 1540s Titian enjoyed an international reputation, painting portraits, mythological scenes, and religious subjects for the Holy Roman emperor Charles V and King Philip II of Spain. Though mannerism succeeded the High Renaissance and then gave way to the 17th-century baroque style, the essential discoveries of the Renaissance underpinned these and every later European movement in painting down to the 20th century.

Painting Techniques and Materials

In the Renaissance most paintings were made either on wooden panels or directly on walls. Artists used tempera, a paint made from egg yolks, and also developed a new material—oil paint. Wall paintings were created using a technique called fresco. At the beginning of the period painters often used costly materials like gold in their work; but as it became increasingly desirable to produce lifelike images, greater emphasis was placed on the skillful use of paint instead.

In the Middle Ages and early years of the Renaissance in the 15th century precious materials were considered as important as the painter's skill. Almost all art was religious and was intended to glorify God. Using costly materials was also a good way for patrons (the people who paid for pictures) to show off their wealth, and they insisted on the most precious materials that they could afford.

Gold was the most valuable of these materials and was widely used by painters. They applied it in thin sheets, or "leafs," or as paint. Gold was used for the backgrounds of pictures, for halos (the circular disks of divine light around the heads of holy figures), and for crowns, jewelry, and intricate patterns on the clothing of the people depicted. The deep blue pigment (color) called aquamarine was used for

the clothes of the Virgin Mary. Aquamarine was only slightly less expensive than gold. In the Renaissance it was made by powdering and soaking a rare stone called lapis lazuli that was imported from the Levant (the area bordering the eastern Mediterranean). Today it is manufactured artificially.

Unlike today, when paint is available ready-made in tubes, in the Middle Ages and the Renaissance artists had to

Above: Saints and angels from **The Coronation of the Virgin** *(about 1450) by the Italian artist Fra Angelico. This detail shows the lavish use of costly materials like gold in the halos, crowns, and clothes.*

make their own materials. Some pigments could be bought ready-made from pharmacies or monasteries, but many had to be prepared by artists themselves. Making and mixing paint was one of the tasks of apprentices (young men training to become artists). They had to grind pigments to a fine powder on stone slabs—often a long and tedious process. When the pigment was ground, it was ready to be mixed with a liquid, called a "binding medium," to create paint.

Two substances were used as the main binding mediums in the Renaissance. In the Middle Ages and early Renaissance egg yolk was the most common binding medium; the paint it produced is called tempera. However, in northern Europe from the 1430s onward plant oil extracted from linseed and walnut began to be used increasingly as a binding medium. By the 16th century this "oil paint" had replaced tempera as the most widely used material.

Right: A 15th-century Flemish picture entitled Saint Luke Painting the Virgin and Child. *Saint Luke was thought to have been a painter and to have made many portraits of the Virgin. For this reason he was the patron saint of artists and was a popular subject of their pictures in the Renaissance. In this painting Saint Luke is shown as if he is working in a 15th-century Flemish workshop. He sits at an easel, holding a palette, as he carefully paints the Virgin's cloak.*

TEMPERA

Tempera paint dries very quickly, and artists mixed only as much as they could use right away. They applied their paint to a prepared wooden panel onto which they had drawn the design of their picture. If gold was to be included, it was applied first, usually over bole (a deep reddish-brown paint) that enhanced the appearance of the thin gold leaf. Next, the artist concentrated on painting any buildings or clothing in the picture. A limited number of colors was used; for example, when a blue cloak was being painted, the artist would mix up the basic blue color, then add varying amounts of white and black to create different tones (lights and darks). Faces and hands were painted last. Often these areas were underpainted with terra verte (green) before a pinker color was applied on top—a procedure that made skin tones look more lifelike.

Artists could build up colors and tones by painting different layers on top of each other, but they were limited by the rapid drying time of the paint. They had to be very steady of hand since mistakes could not be erased, and it was difficult to blend colors.

OIL PAINT

Artists used plant oils in their paints as early as the 11th century, but it was not until the 15th century that plant oils were used as the main binding medium and were exploited for their own particular qualities. Oils dry much slower than tempera and therefore enable artists to spend longer painting tiny details and blending colors. At first artists used a technique similar to that of tempera painting, in which many thin layers, or glazes, were applied to

Above: A 16th-century engraving showing the professions associated with the planet Mercury. At the top right two painters decorate the outside of a building; one prepares paint on a stone slab, while the other paints.

 WOODEN PANELS AND OTHER SUPPORTS

In the Renaissance most pictures that were not painted directly onto walls were made on wooden panels. The wood used depended on the trees that were available locally. Poplar was commonly used in Italy, pine in Germany, and oak in France, Flanders, and Britain, although many other trees were also used. The wood was boiled to remove resin and gum, and to prevent it from splitting and warping later. Any holes were filled with size (a sort of glue), and the wooden panel was covered with several layers of a white, plasterlike material called gesso to create a smooth, hard surface

for the painter to work on. Some northern European artists also specialized in painting on small sheets of metal, such as copper, tin, and silver. Others worked on leather or canvas stretched over wooden frames. Canvas was much cheaper than solid wooden panels, but it was not as highly regarded and was viewed as a support for temporary displays such as the scenery and banners for court entertainments, processions, and plays. It was not until the 17th century that canvas replaced wooden panels as the favored support for paintings.

Right: A preparatory drawing for a fresco by the 15th-century Italian artist Andrea Castagno. It shows Christ at his tomb with two angels. The design was made on a plastered wall in sinopia, a kind of red paint, and the fresco layer was applied on top.

the picture to build up rich colors and tones—this method was used by the Flemish painter Jan van Eyck (about 1395–1441), who was the first artist to develop the use of oils.

Oil paint was perfectly suited to the meticulous, detailed approach of northern European artists, and it was not long before its use spread to Italy. Historians think that it was introduced there either by the southern Italian painter Antonello da Messina (about 1430–1479) or by a northern European artist like Justus of Ghent (active in the 1460s and 1470s) who worked in Italy. Either way, Italian artists would have been able to see new oil paintings from the north in the collections of their patrons. By the 16th century the use of oil paint was widespread in Italy. Some

PIGMENTS AND COLORS

In the Renaissance most pigments came from natural sources, such as rocks, minerals, and plants. In addition to the expensive aquamarine blue, other cheaper blues were made from a more common mineral called azurite and from woad or indigo plants. One of the most widely used yellow pigments was made out of saffron from the stamens of crocus flowers. Vermilion, a bright red, was made from a stone called cinnabar. Black was made by burning wood, bones, or ivory, or from soot. Colors known as "earth pigments" were extracted from different clays.

They included a number of warm, earthy colors such as yellow ocher, Venetian red, burnt sienna (brownish red), and burnt umber (dark brown), as well as terre verte (green). Many other colors were made artificially. For example, red and white lead were produced by the chemical reaction of vinegar on sheets of lead. On the whole, however, painters preferred natural pigments because they were more stable. Artificial pigments were more likely to react with each other and with light, causing them to change color and disintegrate over time.

Italian artists developed a new way of using oil paint called "impasto." Instead of building up pictures from many thin, meticulously painted layers, they applied the paint thickly, with great freedom. The marks of their brushes

---

In Italy by the 16th century frescoes had become one of the most highly regarded forms of art

---

are clearly visible in the paint's surface, and they sometimes mixed different colors together on the picture, rather than the palette. The Venetian painter Titian (1488–1576) was one of the first artists to develop this technique.

FRESCOES

Wall paintings developed as a cheap alternative to costly textile hangings and mosaics. In Italy by the 16th century they had become one of the most highly regarded forms of art. The warm, dry climate there was well suited to wall painting, and artists revived and developed the ancient technique of fresco. Artists in northern Europe also produced murals, although almost none have survived—many were destroyed by the damp climate or painted over by later generations.

To create a fresco, the artist first covered the wall with a layer of rough plaster called *arricciato*. The design for the picture was drawn onto the *arricciato* with charcoal (burned sticks) and sinopia (a red paint). Around 1500 artists also began to use large drawings called cartoons to transfer designs to the wall. A smooth plaster called *intonaco* was then applied to an area of

Left: A detail of Christ's head from Leonardo da Vinci's fresco The Last Supper (1495–1497). It shows the poor state of the picture's surface today, after many flakes of paint have dropped off—the result of Leonardo's experimental techniques.

the picture no bigger than could be painted in one day; this patch of wet plaster was called a *giornato* (from the Italian for "day"). Pigment mixed with water was then applied to this area. As the plaster and pigment dried, they fused to create *buon fresco* (true fresco).

True fresco is a very restrictive method of painting. As with tempera, artists had to work quickly and confidently; and because of the whiteness of the plaster the colors were chalky. To overcome these limitations, artists often added finishing touches in tempera or oil paint when the plaster was dry, a technique known as *fresco al secco*. Many artists experimented by mixing different types of paint with fresco. Leonardo da Vinci (1452–1519) mixed fresco and oils in his wall painting of *The Last Supper* in Milan. However, the mix proved unstable, and bits of paint began to drop off within a few decades of the painting's completion—much of what remains today is the work of restorers.

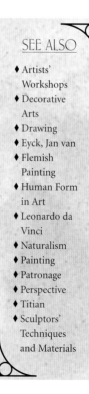

SEE ALSO

♦ Artists' Workshops
♦ Decorative Arts
♦ Drawing
♦ Eyck, Jan van
♦ Flemish Painting
♦ Human Form in Art
♦ Leonardo da Vinci
♦ Naturalism
♦ Painting
♦ Patronage
♦ Perspective
♦ Titian
♦ Sculptors' Techniques and Materials

Palaces and Villas

Left: The Palazzo Farnese in Rome, one of the grandest of the Renaissance palaces. Building work began on the palace in 1513 to a design by Antonio da Sangallo. When the owner, Duke Alessandro Farnese, became Pope Paul III in 1534, the palace was redesigned to be more imposing. After da Sangallo died, Michelangelo finished the work.

Today we usually think of a palace as being the official residence of a king or queen. In Renaissance Italy, however, a palace ("*palazzo*") was any large, imposing town house belonging to a wealthy person or a civic building such as a town hall ("*palazzo pubblico*"). Palaces that were private homes were generally referred to by the name of the family that built them (or later owned them), as in the Palazzo Medici in Florence or the Palazzo Farnese in Rome. A wealthy Renaissance family might also own a similar large residence in the country—it was called a villa.

Grand town houses appeared in Italy long before they did in other parts of Europe. Outside Italy wealth belonged mainly to powerful noblemen who lived in castles surrounded by their land. In Italy, however, towns were more highly developed, and much of the wealth was controlled by bankers and merchants. These people often built imposing buildings in which they both lived and worked—the first palazzi (palaces) usually combined business premises on the first floor with living quarters on the floors above. An excellent early example (built in the late 14th century) is the Palazzo Davanzati in Florence, which is now a museum.

The Palazzo Davanzati is a high, severe-looking building, and this was typical of Renaissance palazzi. Unlike castles, they were not built as fortresses, but they were nevertheless intended to look strong and secure. At the time when the Palazzo Davanzati was built, the political situation in Florence (and in other Italian cities) was unstable, and this sometimes led to riots; a palazzo, as well as being a home, could be used as a place of refuge during bouts of trouble. Even in later periods, when the need for such security was gone, palazzi tended to look sturdy rather than elegant on the outside, although they were often richly decorated inside.

THE MEDICI HOME

The Palazzo Medici in Florence was the home of the Medici family for 100 years from 1444. Brunelleschi's original design was rejected for being too flamboyant, and instead the Medici chose Michelozzo di Bartolommeo as the designer. The Palazzo Medici was one of the most famous palaces of the Renaissance, and its essential features

were imitated in many other buildings. It is a large rectangular structure (rather like a giant box) that fronts directly onto the street, in line with the next-door buildings.

There are three stories, each with orderly rows of windows. Crowning the top edge of the building is a projecting cornice that casts a deep shadow in the bright Italian sunshine. The stonework was deliberately left rough, with deep grooves along the joints to give it a rugged feel. The main doorway leads through a tunnel-like entrance to a square internal courtyard, around which runs a covered arcade like the cloister of a monastery.

PALAZZO FARNESE

About a century later the most majestic of all Renaissance palaces was built—the Palazzo Farnese in Rome. It was begun in 1513; but when Alessandro

FINE FURNITURE

In medieval times Italian woodcarvers were employed to adorn churches. By the 15th century they were using their skills to make furniture for the palazzi and villas of wealthy Italian patrons. Furniture was made from oak,

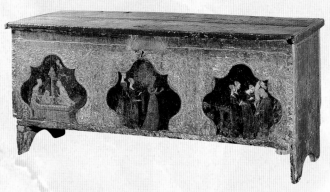

Left: This 15th-century Italian wedding chest is painted with scenes from the Greek myth of the Judgment of Paris.

walnut, cypress, and a new, rare, and expensive wood—ebony. Many ancient Roman techniques were revived, including inlaying the wood surface with patterns made from ivory, mother-of-pearl, different colored woods, and tortoiseshell.

The most expensively decorated piece of Renaissance furniture was the *cassone*, or wedding chest, which was commissioned on the occasion of a

marriage. It was often the most striking piece of furniture in a sparsely furnished bed chamber. *Cassoni* were traditionally made in pairs and sometimes bore the coats of arms of the bride and groom. During the 15th century *cassoni* became increasingly elaborate symbols of the wealth of the families of the marriage partners. Important artists like Botticelli and Ucello were often employed to decorate *cassoni* for the marriages of the Italian elite.

Farnese became Pope Paul III in 1534, it was redesigned on a much more ambitious scale to reflect his new status. The architect was Antonio da Sangallo the Younger, and after his death in 1546 work was continued by Michelangelo. It is even bigger than the Palazzo Medici and more imposing. It has a huge clifflike front 200 ft (60m) wide and 100 ft (30m) high. In spite of this vast bulk, the palazzo has elegance as well as grandeur.

COUNTRY HOUSES

The wealthy people who commissioned palazzi almost always owned land in the country as well as the town, and in the country they built a different type of home—called a villa—as a place to relax in beautiful surroundings (and also as a refuge in times of plague). Like many aspects of the Renaissance, villas were a revival of an ancient Roman idea. Roman villas had usually been the centers of farms, and the first Renaissance villas followed this pattern, although they were sometimes used as hunting lodges rather than for agricultural purposes. During the 16th century, however, villas tended to be built more as status symbols than as working buildings, and many of them were in the suburbs of towns rather than deep in the country.

The Villa Madama (originally the Villa Medici) near Rome, designed by Raphael and begun in about 1516, is an important example of this new type, and it was one of the first villas built to revive the spirit of ancient Roman art. It was commissioned by Cardinal Giulio de Medici, who became Pope Clement VII in 1523. Raphael completed the garden loggia (a roofed space with open sides). It is embellished with exquisite plaster reliefs and painted ornamentation and is one of the most magnificent rooms of the Renaissance period.

Villas were built in most parts of Italy, but predominantly in the north, which was generally more prosperous than the south. Some of the most famous were designed by Andrea

Left: This is the courtyard of the Palazzo Ducale in Urbino. The palazzo was built for Duke Federico da Montefeltro, who ruled Urbino from 1444 to 1482.

THE VILLA D'ESTE GARDEN

From the 16th century many of the major Italian villas had impressive gardens. The most famous was at the Villa d'Este, Tivoli, near Rome. The villa itself is fairly plain, but the gardens are breathtaking. They were laid out mainly between 1560 and 1575 for Cardinal Ippolito d'Este, who went to extraordinary efforts to gain the effects he wanted, even building an aqueduct to provide water for the spectacular fountains. Tivoli was the site of the greatest country estate of the ancient world—Hadrian's Villa. It was excavated during the Renaissance, and much of the sculpture discovered there was displayed in the Villa d'Este gardens.

Above: A vast terrace in the Villa d'Este gardens with a commanding view over the surrounding countryside.

Palladio (1508–1580), the greatest Italian architect of the late 16th century, who worked mainly in and around Vicenza and Venice. His villas tend to be fairly compact, although sometimes there are outbuildings linked by wings to the main block.

ROYAL PALACES

Outside Italy it was not until about 1600 that buildings of comparable form and function to the Italian villa began to appear. There were, however, many impressive palaces built in rural areas as well as in towns. Not surprisingly, the largest and finest palaces were built mainly by royalty. King Henry VIII of England, for example, spent a huge amount on building projects, although most of this work has been destroyed.

The most important palace surviving from Henry's reign is at Hampton Court, near London. It was begun in about 1515 by Cardinal Thomas Wolsey, Henry's chief minister,

and taken over by Henry in 1525; his additions included the great hall, which has a wonderful wooden roof. The palace is built mainly of brick and is essentially in the Gothic style of the Middle Ages. However, Wolsey employed an Italian sculptor, Giovanni da Maiano (about 1486–1542), to make decorative terracotta roundels (small round plaques) featuring portraits of Roman emperors for the outside of the building; they are among the earliest examples of direct Renaissance influence in English architecture.

In France the great royal buildings of the time are generally referred to as châteaus. King Francis I built various rural châteaus, and in Paris he demolished a medieval castle to make way for the Louvre (begun in 1546 as a royal palace and now an art gallery). The Louvre has been greatly enlarged since Francis's time, but the building retains the tone set by the graceful classical style of his architect Pierre Lescot (about 1510–1578).

SEE ALSO

♦ Architecture
♦ Bankers and Banking
♦ Brunelleschi
♦ Este Family
♦ Families
♦ Gardens
♦ Gothic Art
♦ Henry VIII
♦ Houses
♦ Medici Family
♦ Michelangelo
♦ Palladio
♦ Raphael

Timeline

♦ **1305** Giotto begins work on frescoes for the Arena Chapel, Padua—he is often considered the father of Renaissance art.

♦ **1321** Dante publishes the *Divine Comedy*, which has a great influence on later writers.

♦ **1327** Petrarch begins writing the sonnets known as the *Canzoniere*.

♦ **1337** The start of the Hundred Years' War between England and France.

♦ **1353** Boccaccio writes the *Decameron*, an influential collection of 100 short stories.

♦ **1368** The Ming dynasty comes to power in China.

♦ **1377** Pope Gregory XI moves the papacy back to Rome from Avignon, where it has been based since 1309.

♦ **1378** The Great Schism begins: two popes, Urban VI and Clement VII, both lay claim to the papacy.

♦ **1378** English theologian John Wycliffe criticizes the practices of the Roman Catholic church.

♦ **1380** Ivan I of Muscovy defeats the army of the Mongol Golden Horde at the battle of Kulikovo.

♦ **1389** The Ottomans defeat the Serbs at the battle of Kosovo, beginning a new phase of Ottoman expansion.

♦ **1397** Sigismund of Hungary is defeated by the Ottoman Turks at the battle of Nicopolis.

♦ **1397** Queen Margaret of Denmark unites Denmark, Sweden, and Norway under the Union of Kalmar.

♦ **1398** The Mongol leader Tamerlane invades India.

♦ **1399** Henry Bolingbroke becomes Henry IV of England.

♦ **1400** English writer Geoffrey Chaucer dies, leaving his *Canterbury Tales* unfinished.

♦ **1403** In Italy the sculptor Ghiberti wins a competition to design a new set of bronze doors for Florence Cathedral.

♦ **c.1402** The Bohemian preacher Jan Hus begins to attack the corruption of the church.

♦ **1405** The Chinese admiral Cheng Ho commands the first of seven expeditions to the Indian Ocean and East Africa.

♦ **1415** Jan Hus is summoned to the Council of Constance and condemned to death.

♦ **1415** Henry V leads the English to victory against the French at the battle of Agincourt.

♦ **c.1415** Florentine sculptor Donatello produces his sculpture *Saint George*.

♦ **1416** Venice defeats the Ottoman fleet at the battle of Gallipoli, but does not check the Ottoman advance.

♦ **1417** The Council of Constance elects Martin V pope, ending the Great Schism.

♦ **1418** Brunelleschi designs the dome of Florence Cathedral.

♦ **1420** Pope Martin V returns the papacy to Rome, bringing peace and order to the city.

♦ **c.1420** Prince Henry of Portugal founds a school of navigation at Sagres, beginning a great age of Portuguese exploration.

♦ **1422** Charles VI of France dies, leaving his throne to the English king Henry VI. Charles VI's son also claims the throne.

♦ **c.1425** Florentine artist Masaccio paints the *Holy Trinity*, the first painting to use the new science of perspective.

♦ **1429** Joan of Arc leads the French to victory at Orléans; Charles VII is crowned king of France in Reims Cathedral.

♦ **1431** The English burn Joan of Arc at the stake for heresy.

♦ **1433** Sigismund of Luxembourg becomes Holy Roman emperor.

♦ **1434** Cosimo de Medici comes to power in Florence.

♦ **1434** The Flemish artist Jan van Eyck paints the *Arnolfini Marriage* using the newly developed medium of oil paint.

♦ **1439** The Council of Florence proclaims the reunion of the Western and Orthodox churches.

♦ **c.1440** Donatello completes his statue of David—the first life-size bronze sculpture since antiquity.

♦ **1443** Federigo da Montefeltro becomes ruler of Urbino.

♦ **1447** The Milanese people declare their city a republic.

♦ **1450** The condottiere Francesco Sforza seizes control of Milan.

♦ **1450** Fra Angelico paints *The Annunciation* for the monastery of San Marco in Florence.

♦ **1453** Constantinople, capital of the Byzantine Empire, falls to the Ottomans and becomes the capital of the Muslim Empire.

♦ **1453** The French defeat the English at the battle of Castillon, ending the Hundred Years' War.

♦ **1454–1456** Venice, Milan, Florence, Naples, and the papacy form the Italian League to maintain peace in Italy.

♦ **1455** The start of the Wars of the Roses between the Houses of York and Lancaster in England.

♦ **c.1455** The German Johannes Gutenberg develops the first printing press using movable type.

♦ **1456** The Florentine painter Uccello begins work on the *Battle of San Romano*.

♦ **1461** The House of York wins the Wars of the Roses; Edward IV becomes king of England.

♦ **1461** Sonni Ali becomes king of the Songhai Empire in Africa.

♦ **1462** Marsilio Ficino founds the Platonic Academy of Florence— the birthplace of Renaissance Neoplatonism.

♦ **1463** War breaks out between Venice and the Ottoman Empire.

♦ **1465** The Italian painter Mantegna begins work on the Camera degli Sposi in Mantua.

♦ **1467** Civil war breaks out in Japan, lasting for over a century.

♦ **1469** Lorenzo the Magnificent, grandson of Cosimo de Medici, comes to power in Florence.

♦ **1469** The marriage of Isabella I of Castile and Ferdinand V of Aragon unites the two kingdoms.

♦ **1470** The Florentine sculptor Verrocchio completes his *David*.

♦ **1476** William Caxton establishes the first English printing press at Westminster, near London.

♦ **1477** Pope Sixtus IV begins building the Sistine Chapel.

♦ **c.1477** Florentine painter Sandro Botticelli paints the *Primavera*, one of the first large-scale mythological paintings of the Renaissance.

♦ **1478** The Spanish Inquisition is founded in Spain.

♦ **1480** The Ottoman fleet destroys the port of Otranto in south Italy.

♦ **1485** Henry Tudor becomes Henry VII of England—the start of the Tudor dynasty.

♦ **1486** *The Witches' Hammer* is published, a handbook on how to hunt down witches.

♦ **1488** Portuguese navigator Bartholomeu Dias reaches the Cape of Good Hope.

♦ **1491** Missionaries convert King Nzina Nkowu of the Congo to Christianity.

♦ **1492** The Spanish monarchs conquer Granada, the last Moorish territory in Spain.

♦ **1492** Christopher Columbus lands in the Bahamas, claiming the territory for Spain.

♦ **1492** Henry VII of England renounces all English claims to the French throne.

♦ **1493** The Hapsburg Maximilian becomes Holy Roman emperor.

♦ **1494** Charles VIII of France invades Italy, beginning four decades of Italian wars.

♦ **1494** In Italy Savonarola comes to power in Florence.

♦ **1494** The Treaty of Tordesillas divides the non-Christian world between Spain and Portugal.

♦ **1495** Leonardo da Vinci begins work on *The Last Supper* .

♦ **1495** Spain forms a Holy League with the Holy Roman emperor and expels the French from Naples.

♦ **1498** Portuguese navigator Vasco da Gama reaches Calicut, India.

♦ **1498** German artist Dürer creates the *Apocalypse* woodcuts.

♦ **1500** Portuguese navigator Pedro Cabral discovers Brazil.

♦ **c.1500–1510** Dutch painter Hieronymus Bosch paints *The Garden of Earthly Delights*.

♦ **c.1502** Italian architect Donato Bramante designs the Tempietto Church in Rome.

♦ **1503** Leonardo da Vinci begins painting the *Mona Lisa*.

♦ **1504** Michelangelo finishes his statue of David, widely seen as a symbol of Florence.

♦ **c.1505** Venetian artist Giorgione paints *The Tempest*.

♦ **1506** The Italian architect Donato Bramante begins work on rebuilding Saint Peter's, Rome.

♦ **1508** Michelangelo begins work on the ceiling of the Sistine Chapel in the Vatican.

♦ **1509** Henry VIII ascends the throne of England.

♦ **1509** The League of Cambrai defeats Venice at the battle of Agnadello.

♦ **1510–1511** Raphael paints *The School of Athens* in the Vatican.

♦ **1511** The French are defeated at the battle of Ravenna in Italy and are forced to retreat over the Alps.

♦ **1513** Giovanni de Medici becomes Pope Leo X.

♦ **1515** Thomas Wolsey becomes lord chancellor of England.

♦ **1515** Francis I becomes king of France. He invades Italy and captures Milan.

♦ **c.1515** German artist Grünewald paints the *Isenheim Altarpiece*.

♦ **1516** Charles, grandson of the emperor Maximilian I, inherits the Spanish throne as Charles I.

♦ **1516** Thomas More publishes his political satire *Utopia*.

♦ **1516** Dutch humanist Erasmus publishes a more accurate version of the Greek New Testament.

♦ **1517** Martin Luther pins his 95 theses on the door of the castle church in Wittenburg.

♦ **1519** Charles I of Spain becomes Holy Roman emperor Charles V.

♦ **1519–1521** Hernán Cortés conquers Mexico for Spain.

♦ **1520** Henry VIII of England and Francis I of France meet at the Field of the Cloth of Gold to sign a treaty of friendship.

♦ **1520** Portuguese navigator Ferdinand Magellan discovers a route to the Indies around the tip of South America.

♦ **1520** Süleyman the Magnificent becomes ruler of the Ottoman Empire, which now dominates the eastern Mediterranean.

♦ **1520–1523** Titian paints *Bacchus and Ariadne* for Alfonso d'Este.

♦ **1521** Pope Leo X excommuicates Martin Luther.

♦ **1521** The emperor Charles V attacks France, beginning a long period of European war.

♦ **1522** Ferdinand Magellan's ship the *Victoria* is the first to sail around the world.

♦ **1523–1525** Huldrych Zwingli sets up a Protestant church at Zurich in Switzerland.

♦ **1525** In Germany the Peasants' Revolt is crushed, and its leader, Thomas Münzer, is executed.

♦ **1525** The emperor Charles V defeats the French at the battle of Pavia and takes Francis I prisoner.

♦ **1525** William Tyndale translates the New Testament into English.

♦ **1526** The Ottoman Süleyman the Magnificent defeats Hungary at the battle of Mohács.

♦ **1526** Muslim Mongol leader Babur invades northern India and establishes the Mogul Empire.

♦ **c.1526** The Italian artist Correggio paints the *Assumption of the Virgin* in Parma Cathedral.

♦ **1527** Charles V's armies overrun Italy and sack Rome.

♦ **1527–1530** Gustavus I founds a Lutheran state church in Sweden.

♦ **1528** Italian poet and humanist Baldassare Castiglione publishes *The Courtier*.

♦ **1529** The Ottoman Süleyman the Magnificent lays siege to Vienna, but eventually retreats.

♦ **1530** The Catholic church issues the "Confutation," attacking Luther and Protestantism.

♦ **1531** The Protestant princes of Germany form the Schmalkaldic League.

♦ **1531–1532** Francisco Pizarro conquers Peru for Spain.

♦ **1532** Machiavelli's *The Prince* is published after his death.

♦ **1533** Henry VIII of England rejects the authority of the pope and marries Anne Boleyn.

♦ **1533** Anabaptists take over the city of Münster in Germany.

♦ **1533** Christian III of Denmark founds the Lutheran church of Denmark.

♦ **1534** Paul III becomes pope and encourages the growth of new religious orders such as the Jesuits.

♦ **1534** Luther publishes his German translation of the Bible.

♦ **1534** The Act of Supremacy declares Henry VIII supreme head of the Church of England.

♦ **c.1535** Parmigianino paints the mannerist masterpiece *Madonna of the Long Neck*.

♦ **1535–1536** The Swiss city of Geneva becomes Protestant and expels the Catholic clergy.

♦ **1536** Calvin publishes *Institutes of the Christian Religion*, which sets out his idea of predestination.

♦ **1536** Pope Paul III sets up a reform commission to examine the state of the Catholic church.

♦ **1537** Hans Holbein is appointed court painter to Henry VIII of England.

♦ **1539** Italian painter Bronzino begins working for Cosimo de Medici the Younger in Florence.

♦ **1539** Ignatius de Loyola founds the Society of Jesus (the Jesuits).

♦ **1541** John Calvin sets up a model Christian city in Geneva.

♦ **1543** Andreas Vesalius publishes *On the Structure of the Human Body*, a handbook of anatomy based on dissections.

♦ **1543** Polish astronomer Copernicus's *On the Revolutions of the Heavenly Spheres* proposes a sun-centered universe.

♦ **1544** Charles V and Francis I of France sign the Truce of Crespy.

♦ **1545** Pope Paul III organizes the Council of Trent to counter the threat of Protestantism.

♦ **1545** Spanish explorers find huge deposits of silver in the Andes Mountains of Peru.

♦ **1547** Charles V defeats the Protestant Schmalkaldic League at the Battle of Mühlberg.

♦ **1547** Ivan IV "the Terrible" declares himself czar of Russia.

♦ **1548** Titian paints the equestrian portrait *Charles V after the Battle of Mühlberg*.

♦ **1548** Tintoretto paints *Saint Mark Rescuing the Slave*.

♦ **1550** Italian Georgio Vasari publishes his *Lives of the Artists*.

♦ **1553** Mary I of England restores the Catholic church.

♦ **1554** Work begins on the Cathedral of Saint Basil in Red Square, Moscow.

♦ **1555** At the Peace of Augsburg Charles V allows the German princes to determine their subjects' religion.

♦ **1556** Ivan IV defeats the last Mongol khanates. Muscovy now dominates the Volga region.

♦ **1556** Philip II becomes king of Spain.

♦ **1559** Elizabeth I of England restores the Protestant church.

♦ **1562** The Wars of Religion break out in France.

♦ **1565** Flemish artist Pieter Bruegel the Elder paints *Hunters in the Snow*.

♦ **1565** Italian architect Palladio designs the Villa Rotunda, near Vicenza.

♦ **1566** The Dutch revolt against the Spanish over the loss of political and religious freedoms:

Philip II of Spain sends 10,000 troops under the duke of Alba to suppress the revolt.

♦ **1569** Flemish cartographer Mercator produces a world map using a new projection.

♦ **1571** Philip II of Spain and an allied European force defeat the Ottomans at the battle of Lepanto.

♦ **1572** In Paris, France, a Catholic mob murders thousands of Huguenots in the Saint Bartholomew's Day Massacre.

♦ **1572** Danish astronomer Tycho Brahe sees a new star.

♦ **1573** Venetian artist Veronese paints the *Feast of the House of Levi*.

♦ **1579** The seven northern provinces of the Netherlands form the Union of Utrecht.

♦ **1580** Giambologna creates his mannerist masterpiece *Flying Mercury*.

♦ **1585** Henry III of France bans Protestantism in France; civil war breaks out again in the War of the Three Henrys.

♦ **1586** El Greco, a Greek artist active in Spain, paints the *Burial of Count Orgaz*.

♦ **1587** Mary, Queen of Scots, is executed by Elizabeth I of England.

♦ **c.1587** Nicholas Hilliard paints the miniature *Young Man among Roses*.

♦ **1588** Philip II of Spain launches his great Armada against England —but the fleet is destroyed.

♦ **1589** Henry of Navarre becomes king of France as Henry IV.

♦ **1592–1594** Tintoretto paints *The Last Supper*.

♦ **1596** Edmund Spencer publishes the *Faerie Queene*, glorifying Elizabeth I as "Gloriana."

♦ **1598** Henry IV of France grants Huguenots and Catholics equal political rights.

♦ **1598** In England the Globe Theater is built on London's south bank; it stages many of Shakespeare's plays.

♦ **1600–1601** Caravaggio paints *The Crucifixion of Saint Peter*, an early masterpiece of baroque art.

♦ **1603** Elizabeth I of England dies and is succeeded by James I, son of Mary, Queen of Scots.

♦ **1610** Galileo's *The Starry Messenger* supports the sun-centered model of the universe.

♦ **1620** The Italian painter Artemisia Gentileschi paints *Judith and Holofernes*.

Glossary

Acoustic A term used to describe musical instruments that produce sound that is not electronically modified.

A.D. The letters A.D. stand for the Latin Anno Domini, which means "in the year of our Lord." Dates with these letters written after them are measured forward from the year Christ was born.

Administrator A person whose job involves the day-to-day running of an organization, like a business or government department.

Altarpiece A painting or sculpture placed behind an altar in a church.

Apprentice Someone (usually a young person) legally bound to a craftsman for a number of years in order to learn a craft.

Basilica An ancient Roman building or early Christian church that is rectangular in shape with a semicircular end; also a Roman Catholic church that has special ceremonial privileges.

B.C. Short for "Before Christ." Dates with these letters after them are measured backward from the year of Christ's birth.

Bureaucracy A system of government that relies on a body of officials and usually involves much paperwork and many regulations.

Cardinal An official of the Catholic church, highest in rank below the pope. The cardinals elect the pope.

Classical A term used to describe the civilizations of ancient Greece and Rome, and any later art and architecture based on ancient Greek and Roman examples.

Cloister A roofed passage running around a courtyard that has a solid wall on the outside and is open to the courtyard on the inside—the inside "wall" is often made up of rows of columns with large openings between them. It was part of the buildings that made up monasteries and usually connected the church to the monks' living quarters.

Conquistador Someone who led the Spanish conquest of America, particularly of Peru and Mexico, in the 16th century.

Cornice A molded horizontal strip at the top of an architectural feature. In classical architecture the term is often specifically applied to part of the carved band (the "entablature") that is supported by columns.

Emissary A person who acts as an agent or representative for another person.

Equestrian A term used to describe something relating to a person on horseback. For example, an equestrian sculpture is a sculpture portraying a soldier or leader on horseback.

Euthanasia Mercy killing, or assisting an incurably ill person to die to save them suffering further pain.

Fortress A strong building built to protect people and land from enemy attack.

Fresco A type of painting that is usually used for decorating walls and ceilings in which pigments (colors) are painted into wet plaster.

Fret One of a series of ridges that run under the strings of musical instruments like the guitar. Different notes are produced by pressing the strings down between the various frets.

Guerilla A person who fights for a cause using irregular methods, such as sabotaging the operations of their enemy.

Guild An association of merchants or craftsmen organized to protect the interests of its members and to regulate the quality of their goods and services.

Holy Roman emperor The ruler of a large collection of semiindependent states, many of them covering lands in present-day Germany, known as the Holy Roman Empire. In the Renaissance the strongest emperors came from the Hapsburg family, although they drew most their power from their own wealth and territories rather than from the empire.

Humanism A new way of thinking about human life that characterized the Renaissance. It was based on the study of "humanities"— that is, ancient Greek and Roman texts, history, and philosophy—and stressed the importance of developing rounded, cultured people.

Laity or lay people Anyone who is not of the clergy.

Loggia A room, or an ornamental garden building, that is open on one or more sides.

Mercenary A soldier who will fight for any employer in return for money.

Meridian A line on a map or globe of the world that runs all around the earth's surface to connect the north and south poles.

Opera A drama set to music with singers and orchestra.

Ore A type of rock that contains a valuable material, like silver or gold, that can be extracted from it.

Patron Someone who orders and pays for a work of art.

Patronage The act of ordering and paying for a work of art.

Perspective A technique that allows artists to create the impression of three-dimensional space in their pictures. Near objects are made to appear larger, and far objects are shown as smaller.

Relief A type of sculpture in which the design is carved to stand out from a flat background.

Roundel A circular panel, window, or frame. It was a popular decorative feature in Renaissance buildings.

Theology The study of religious faith, practice, and experience.

Treatise A book or long essay about the principles, or rules, of a particular subject.

Vernacular The language of the ordinary people of a country, rather than a literary or formal language like Latin.

Further Reading

Ackroyd, Peter. *The Life of Thomas More.* New York: Anchor Books, 1999.

Allen, Michael. *The Platonism of Marsilio Ficino.* Berkeley, CA: University of California Press, 1984.

Atlas, Allan W. *Renaissance Music: Music in Western Europe, 1400–1600.* New York: W.W. Norton, 1998.

Bator, Robert. *Daily Life in Ancient and Modern Istanbul.* Minneapolis, MN: Runestone Press, 2000.

Beck, James H., Antonio Paolucci, and Bruno Santi. *Michelangelo: The Medici Chapel.* London: Thames & Hudson, 1994.

Beck, James. *Italian Renaissance Painting.* Cologne, Germany: Könemann, 1999.

Brown, Howard Mayer, and Louise K. Stein. *Music in the Renaissance.* Upper Saddle River, NJ: Prentice Hall, 1999.

Christiansen, Keith. *Andrea Mantegna: Padua and Mantua.* New York: George Braziller, 1994.

De Vecchi, Pierluigi. *Michelangelo: The Vatican Frescoes.* New York: Abbeville Press, 1997.

Evdokimov, Paul. *The Art of the Icon: A Theology of Beauty.* Redondo Beach, CA: Oakwood Publications, 1989.

Giudici, Vittorio. *The Sistine Chapel: Its History and Masterpieces.* New York: Peter Bedrick Books, 2000.

Gombrich, E. H. *The Story of Art.* London: Phaidon Press, 1995.

Goodwin, Jason. *Lords of the Horizons: A History of the Ottoman Empire.* New York: Henry Holt, 1999.

Gurrieri, Francesco. *Palaces of Florence.* New York: Rizzoli, 1996.

Gutierrez, Gustavo. *Las Casas: In Search of the Poor of Jesus Christ.* Maryknoll, NY: Orbis Books, 1993.

Hall, Marcia B. *Color and Meaning: Practice and Theory in Renaissance Painting.* Cambridge, UK: Cambridge University Press, 1992.

Hersey, George L. *Pythagorean Palaces: Magic and Architecture in the Italian Renaissance.* Ithaca, NY: Cornell University Press, 1976.

Hibbard, Howard. *Michelangelo.* New York: Harper & Row, 1985.

Itzkowitz, Norman. *Ottoman Empire and Islamic Tradition.* Chicago, IL: University of Chicago Press, 1980.

Kent, Deborah. *Amsterdam.* New York: Children's Press, 1997.

Llewellyn, Nigel. *Funeral Monuments in Post-Reformation England.* Cambridge, UK: Cambridge University Press, 2001.

Lord Kinross. *Ottoman Centuries: The Rise and Fall of the Turkish Empire.* New York: William Morrow, 1988.

Mak, Geert. *Amsterdam.* Cambridge, MA: Harvard University Press, 1999.

Marius, Richard. *Thomas More: A Biography.* New York: Knopf, 1984.

Montagu, Jeremy. *The World of Medieval and Renaissance Musical Instruments.* Newton Abbott, UK: David & Charles, 1976.

Morrison, Taylor. *Antonio's Apprenticeship: Painting a Fresco in Renaissance Italy.* New York: Holiday House, 1996.

Munman, Robert. *Sienese Renaissance Tomb Monuments.* Philadelphia, PA: American Philosophical Society, 1993.

Nash, Jane. *Veiled Images: Titian's Mythological Paintings for Philip II.* Philadelphia, PA: Art Alliance Press, 1986.

Nava, Simonetta. *Painting in Renaissance Italy.* New York: Rizzoli, 2000.

Paoletti, John T. *Art in Renaissance Italy.* New York: Harry N. Abrams, 1997.

Paolucci, Antonio. *Michelangelo: The Pietàs.* Milan, Italy: Skira, 2000.

Parry, J. H. *The Age of Reconnaissance.* Berkeley, CA: University of California Press, 1981.

Parry, J. H. *Europe and a Wider World, 1415–1715.* London: Hutchinson, 1966.

Partridge, Loren. *The Art of Renaissance Rome: 1400–1600.* New York: Harry N. Abrams, 1996.

Reid, Jane Davidson, and Chris Rohmann. *The Oxford Guide to Classical Mythology in the Arts, 1300–1900s.* Oxford: Oxford University Press, 1993.

Richmond, Robin. *Michelangelo and the Creation of the Sistine Chapel.* New York: Crescent Books, 1995.

Sala, Charles. *Michelangelo: Sculptor, Painter, Architect.* Paris: Terrail, 1997.

Schama, Simon. *The Embarrassment of Riches: Dutch Culture in the Golden Age.* New York: Vintage Books, 1997.

Schrade, Leo. *Monteverdi: Creator of Modern Music.* New York: Da Capo Press, 1979.

Simmons, Dawn Langley. *William, Father of the Netherlands.* Chicago, IL: Rand McNally, 1969.

Stanley, Diane. *Michelangelo.* New York: HarperCollins Juvenile Books, 2000.

Strong, Roy. *The English Renaissance Miniature.* London: Thames & Hudson, 1983.

Wallis, Richard T. *Neoplatonism.* London: Duckworth, 1995.

Ware, Timothy. *The Orthodox Church.* New York: Penguin USA, 1993.

Westermann, Mariet. *A Worldly Art: The Dutch Republic 1585–1718.* New York: Harry N. Abrams, 1996.

Wilson, Derek A. *England in the Age of Thomas More.* London: Hart-Davis MacGibbon, 1978.

Wundram, Manfred. *Painting of the Renaissance.* New York: Taschen, 1997.

Zorzi, Alvise, and Paolo Marton. *Venetian Palaces.* New York: Rizzoli, 1990.

WEBSITES

World history site
www.historyworld.net

BBC Online: History
www.bbc.co.uk/history

The Webmuseum's tour of the Renaissance
www.oir.ucf.edu/wm/paint/glo/renaissance/

Virtual time travel tour of the Renaissance
library.thinkquest.org/3588/Renaissance/

The Renaissance
www.learner.org/exhibits/renaissance

National Gallery of Art—tour of 16th-century Italian paintings
www.nga.gov/collection/gallery/ita16.htm

Uffizi Art Gallery, Florence
musa.uffizi.firenze.it/welcomeE.html

Database of Renaissance artists
www.artcyclopedia.com/index.html

Set Index

Numbers in **bold type** are volume numbers.

Page numbers in *italics* refer to pictures or their captions.

MAPS
The maps in this book show the locations of cities, states, and empires of the Renaissance period. However, for the sake of clarity, present-day place names are often used.